Garden Landscaping
Manual

First published in May 2011
Reprinted November 2011

British Library Cataloguing in Publication Data
A catalogue record for this book is available from
the British Library

ISBN 978 1 84425 972 4

Library of Congress Catalog Card no. 2010934898

Published by Haynes Publishing,
Sparkford, Yeovil, Somerset BA22 7JJ, UK
Tel: 01963 442030 Fax: 01963 440001
Int. tel: +44 1963 442030 Int. fax: +44 1963 440001
E-mail: sales@haynes.co.uk
Website: www.haynes.co.uk

Haynes North America Inc.
861 Lawrence Drive, Newbury Park,
California 91320, USA

Printed and bound in the UK by Gomer Press Limited,
Llandysul Enterprise Park, Llandysul, Ceredigion SA44 4JL

Credits

Author:	Paul Wagland
Project Manager:	Louise McIntyre
Copy editor:	Ian Heath
Page design:	Richard Parsons
Index:	Peter Nicholson

Garden Landscaping
Manual

CONTENTS

INTRODUCTION

With today's hectic pace of life, our gardens have become much more than they once were. No longer are they simply a practical necessity for drying clothes, growing veg or exercising kids and pets. Neither are they purely ornamental, as the grounds of well-healed households once were. Instead they must fulfil a wide range of roles, from the traditional ones just mentioned to those which allow us to make more of our time; relaxing, entertaining, working outdoors and even improving the value of our houses. This extended list of demands has meant that garden design has changed in recent years. Once, well-groomed collections of beautiful and unusual plants were at the top of the typical gardener's wish list (and this, of course, still applies to a few traditionalists). Now, however, space in which to relax and entertain is the priority, often twinned with a desire for a low-maintenance arrangement that doesn't place too great a demand on the owner's time. We want gardens we can live in, not just utilise or admire, and this is why we need good landscaping.

What is landscaping?

It's something of a shame that the word landscaping has become associated with large-scale, publicly funded and often rather bland and disappointing schemes outside office blocks and apartment buildings. Its real meaning is much broader than that; it is the process of designing and creating outdoor space. The implication is that this space will be both beautiful and practical, and this is a very important balance to achieve. On the domestic scale, whether you're talking about a tiny yard or several acres of rolling grounds, this must be your constant aim. Making a useful, usable space into something inviting, or even sensual, is not as difficult as you might think, but it does take careful thought.

Chapter 1 is all about planning and design; even if you know what you want and where you want it, it's worth treating this as a starting point unless you're sure you already possess the relevant skills. Make your mistakes on paper and they'll cost you much less than making them for real. As well as enabling you to develop an idea into much more than you first imagined, the planning process is also a great way to get to know your garden; you'll become familiar with every corner, every plant and every feature. There are few gardens more enjoyable than the one we have created ourselves from the ground up.

Making it work

If you're planning to spend money on improvements you'll want to be sure you see the benefits. In other words you want to make changes that really improve your time spent outdoors, and, indeed, which tempt you outside to make the most of them. One way to approach this is to treat the garden as an extension of the house, as if the back door were just opening into another room – albeit one without a

ceiling! In professional circles this is sometimes referred to as 'inside-outside', or just 'bringing the garden in'.

The trick is to blur the boundaries between inside and out, making the transition less of an event in itself. A high-budget example might be the replacement of a rear wall with floor-to-ceiling glazing, although good-quality patio doors would be within the reach of more people. If such changes are impractical or out of your price range, simply keeping the approach to the back door (from either direction) clear of furniture and other obstacles can make a big difference.

Materials also have a big role to play. If you have paving right by the door from the house to the garden, you'll feel more comfortable moving between the two. Likewise, any form of shelter, be it an elegant conservatory or just a simple timber pergola, can create an intermediary zone – a more gentle change in environment

A garden for living in

Even the smallest patio or sun terrace gives you somewhere practical to entertain friends, and positioned just outside the kitchen door such robust materials as timber and stone are a great way to lessen that distinction between inside and outside. Your garden should be arranged so that you can make more use of the outside space in all weather; this can even help keep muddy footprints out of the house. All types, sizes and styles of garden can be improved with a little creative effort, and if you choose your design and materials carefully changes should blend seamlessly with other elements of the garden.

It is crucial at the design stage for you to be realistic about what you want from your plot. If you have the inclination to be a vegetable gardener, but not the time, then it's worth saving the inclination for the future.

Adding value

Thinking about the long-term, it's worth considering the added value that a well-designed and useful garden, or even a courtyard patio or terrace, can bring to your home. After all, our houses represent the single biggest financial investment most of us are ever likely to make, so it makes sense to give that investment the attention it deserves. Here's the key point; depending on the location, estate agents and property experts estimate a good garden can add anywhere between 5% and 15% to the overall value of a house. Think about the price of the average house these days and you'll see this could represent a significant return on the investment of time, money and effort involved in a full garden makeover. It is perhaps not surprising that houses in inner-city locations, where green space is at a premium, are particularly enhanced by an inviting garden. It's certainly worth thinking about when you assign a budget to any such project – far from being an expense, this is money that will be returned to you in the future when you come to sell.

Another aspect of this is that houses which appeal on more than the basic level tend to sell more quickly, which is all-important when the housing market is less than booming. It's hard to quantify this advantage, but the 'wow factor' provided by a beautiful garden could really set your house apart from the competition.

If your budget is tight, there are many ways of keeping costs low while still maximising the results. Some projects can be taken on in stages (giving the bank account a chance to recover), while others may only require inexpensive materials and little or no professional help.

Assessing your capabilities

The fact that you've bought this book suggests you're willing to try your hand at DIY. This might not mean you're hugely experienced, or even that you know where to start, but, as with so many things in life, just deciding to 'have a go' is often the most important step. Garden landscaping is not a hugely technical subject, in fact quite the reverse, and hopefully this book will give you all you need to turn your ideas into practical realities. You'll quickly develop skills you never thought you'd have, and see your achievements take shape day by day.

My advice to any novice DIYer is simply to get started

– it's almost always easier than you think. The one caveat here has to do with the practical nature of landscaping work. While it might not be complicated it is often physically demanding – building a patio, for example, may require you to remove several tonnes of earth, then replace them with tonnes of crushed concrete, sand and cement. Large paving slabs can weigh too much for one person to safely lift, and prolonged periods of unfamiliar work can leave you very sore and tired. Read the section on 'Working safely' in Chapter 2, then decide for yourself what you can manage alone and where you'll need help.

Using this book

Which parts of this book you use are dependent on your existing knowledge and experience. If you already have some design skills you may want to skip to Chapter 2, where we take a look at tools and materials, while the more accomplished DIY enthusiast may choose to read-up on design in Chapter 1 and then go on to some of the practical projects described in Chapters 3 and 5 onwards. The book is arranged to allow you to concentrate on the areas that most interest you, with all aspects of hard and soft landscaping, garden structures and water features grouped together in their own sections.

Whatever your goals and circumstances, the aim of this book is to provide you with the inspiration and knowledge required to achieve a great result.

GARDEN LANDSCAPING

PLANNING AND DESIGN

1

Planning and design

Unless you're very talented or remarkably lucky, the real success of your landscaping projects will be decided at the design stage. Every aspect of how, where and why you make changes to the existing garden should be carefully considered and ideally written down or drawn. When you're working with such long-lived materials as concrete and stone it's wise to make your decisions in advance of construction and, unless circumstances change, to stick to them. It's much less frustrating to realise at the planning stage that your new patio won't get enough sun than it is to do so once the thing is built.

If this is to be a family garden you could ask every member of the family to write a list of what they'd like to do there, and how they see the garden being used. If you choose to do this, you need to make sure that people are realistic about their expectations, and don't let a multitude of ideas get lost in each other's shadow. Design by committee is almost never a good idea, but listening to other people and developing an inclusive plan is sure to make the contributors more likely to enjoy the finished product.

It may also be possible to give family members 'ownership' of a certain aspect or area of the garden. Perhaps the children can help to design a play area with rope swings, climbing frame or tree house. If one person is a vegetable grower they'll be delighted to be able to choose how that part of the garden is laid out, perhaps with beds running north to south to give their plants even exposure to the sun through the day.

Assessing a garden

Before you make a start on any grand design, the first thing you should do is take note of what you have already. There's no such thing as a blank canvas in this situation – your existing garden may be full of plants and features, or it may be a plain, level square of turf. Either way there are things you need to know before you make decisions about how the garden will end up. A garden designer once told me I should study a plot for a year before I started to design any changes, so that I can experience the full range of seasons and weather. Now, I can't say I have the patience for that, and it's usually not practical, but it shows you how vital it is to understand the existing landscape.

Perhaps the most important things to consider are aspect and exposure. These two factors can determine, or at least strongly influence, what design element goes where, which materials you use, how high your fences, plants and structures should be, and even what times of day you'll be able to enjoy your garden most. For those who aren't familiar with the terms, they can be defined as follows:

Aspect

Aspect is related to direction (north, south, east or west), but on a more localised, personal scale. You should firstly use a compass to determine which way the garden 'faces', in other words the direction in which it's most open to the sky. This is often (but by no means always) away from the back wall of the house and is perhaps the single most important factor affecting your design.

In the Northern Hemisphere a garden that faces south will receive the most sun throughout the day, and will therefore be bright and warm (but possibly inhospitably so in high summer). Gardens that face north are more challenging – they're quite likely to be overshadowed and cool, and therefore able to support a different range of plants.

A westerly aspect will give you shady mornings and sun through late afternoon into the evening (nice for a glass of wine after work) and will make the most of sunny weather, as the garden warms up through the day. East-facing gardens benefit from morning sunshine, but this is often not very warming as the air temperature falls through the night.

Further to your compass reading, make a note of the surrounding buildings, trees and other tall objects. These will cast shadows of their own and can therefore influence the final positions of decks, patios and other seating areas. It's a good idea to go outside at different times of day and make notes about where the shadows are falling. This will give you a clearer picture of the sunny spots and those that are more shady, so that you know how to take advantage of both.

Exposure

This is in many ways related to aspect, because it depends to a degree on surrounding buildings and other obstacles, but has less to do with sunlight and more to do with other types of weather. Chief among these are wind and cold, both of which can harm your plants, not to mention your enjoyment of the outside space. We're probably all familiar with the parts of our gardens that suffer in the wind – often it's a 'pinch point' between the house and another vertical object like a garage or a fence. Sometimes it's simply at a corner of the house where the wind tends to whip by.

While you're generally unable to do very much to alter the aspect of your garden, you can reduce wind exposure by using sensible planting, garden structures (for example trellis panels) and other aspects of your design. An interesting fact is that a permeable obstacle such as a hedge or an open fence will do more to improve conditions in windy weather than will a solid structure like a wall or a shed. This is because the wind is deflected, filtered and slowed down, rather than forced over or around a large object (which will often create a vortex of rapidly moving air). The other important element of exposure is the cold, and this is

particularly important when choosing what plants to grow. More tender varieties won't appreciate exposure to the cold, and will do better in a sheltered position against a warm wall. Consequently tougher species should be chosen for colder spots such as a northerly aspect with little or no surrounding shelter, or where the ground is lower and therefore more prone to frost.

Exposure will vary somewhat through the year, but you should be able to extrapolate for other seasons – shadows are short in summer and long in winter, the worst of the winds and other weather will commonly come in autumn and winter, and usually from the same directions (south-west in the UK, although the coldest winds come from the north-east).

There are also many other points to consider at this early stage, and the skill of the designer is in assessing the value of each and reacting to all of them in what is overall the most beneficial manner. Here are the main ones to remember:

Privacy

This is hugely important if you want to be able to enjoy some personal time in the garden. Nobody wants to be overlooked while they sunbathe or get lost in a good book, so you should think about the positioning of the windows of neighbouring houses in relation to your plot. Will the person at Number 12 be able to see across your patio while you eat, or will your neighbours be able to overhear conversations through the fence? You'll find it hard to relax in a garden that doesn't feel private.

Topography

This word might sound intimidating, but it simply means the lie of the land. Does your plot slope in one or more directions, and is that slope consistent from one end of the plot to another, or does it roll? Are there any high points or hollows? Although a totally flat and level site is probably the easiest to work with, any decent slope can give you all kinds of design opportunities such as raised decks, terraced beds, even streams and waterfalls. These features can transform a garden and make the increased technical challenges worthwhile.

Soil type

The sort of soil you have in your garden probably doesn't strike you as the most important thing to measure before you start designing. However, it will influence your choice of plants, and possibly also the method of any hard landscaping construction. The acidity (or pH level) of the soil is best determined with a soil testing kit – most involve dissolving a soil sample in water, then dipping indicator paper into the solution. This will tell you if you have acid or alkaline ground, and will therefore inform your choice of plants. The make-up of the soil is also important, as some soils are more stable than others, so may be the deciding factor in the choice between different types or dimensions of foundations. It's a simple thing to assess – pick up a lump of damp soil and squeeze it. If it slips and slides between your fingers it has a high clay content; if it crumbles quickly and feels gritty it's sandy. More complex and comprehensive tests are possible, but often a quick chat with neighbouring gardeners will be enough to confirm your results.

Drainage

Drainage is often related to soil type, with clay-rich soils draining more slowly than sandy ones, particularly if the former have been compressed by heavy traffic. It will have an effect on the plants you can grow, including how healthy a lawn will be, and in very poorly-drained ground it might be better to use a concrete foundation than rely on sunken timber posts to hold up

fences and garden buildings. It can be difficult to measure drainage, particularly in fine weather, so use your common sense, and ask neighbours for their thoughts.

Physical features

Any garden buildings, boundaries, services or other existing objects in the garden should also be assessed. Do they need to stay where they are, or would they be better positioned elsewhere? If they're old and past their best, can they be renovated or should they be removed? Some features can be converted from one use into an entirely different one – a good way of adding character to your garden.

Taking all these considerations into account, you should be able to make a reasonable assessment of your plot in two or three days of observation, and this will help you decide what you want to keep, what needs to be removed, and what is missing. Make plenty of notes and sketches, then draw a detailed plan of the garden as it is now.

Surveying and measuring

The first step towards creating a plan of the existing plot is to measure and record the dimensions. Start with the boundaries and work inwards, double-checking each measurement as you take it. The time you invest at this early stage will be rewarded when you come to build, as accurate information will allow you to buy the right quantities of materials and will also facilitate straightforward construction. A surveyor's tape measure, usually 30m or 50m long, is the ideal tool for this task. You'll need the help of at least one other person to hold the tape taut and horizontal (a curved or diagonal line will be longer) and perhaps to write down the measurements as you call them out. A 5m tape measure is also useful for assessing garden buildings and other, smaller details.

Remember that not all corners are square! Use a large carpenter's square (sometimes called a builder's square) to measure every corner of your plot. Even small differences from a 90° angle can make a big difference to the finished project when the overall distances are large.

Don't forget that you're designing in three dimensions, so you'll need a long spirit level to detect any changes in height. To quantify any such change, measure horizontally from the top of the slope, out to a given distance – let's say 2m. At this point, push a straight bamboo cane into the ground and make sure it's vertical. The distance from the ground, up the cane, to the point where the horizontal measurement intersects will give you the change in level per two metres. Let's say this is a drop of 20cm; you can convert this to a ratio of 1:10. It can be handy to know the length of your spirit level – a 2m-long level would make the above task very easy to perform.

It isn't easy to record changes of level on a standard two-dimensional plan, but you should at least make a note of your measurements, and in complicated cases you should draw a cross-section showing how the gradient changes. The tools mentioned here are discussed in more detail in Chapter 2. Small changes in level can be corrected by moving earth from the high ground to the low, but you don't want to do too much of this as the amount of work involved will quickly mount up. Even if you have access to a mini digger, flattening a sloping site will take time. What's more, you must consider

how much higher the ground will be at the base of the slope (will boundary fences or plants be buried?), and how much lower at the top (will the step down from a kitchen door be too high?). All in all it's better to consider the slope as a part of the garden and design around it. Small excavations, such as flattening the site of a patio, are much easier to manage.

Working to scale

While the measurements you take 'in the field' might be scribbled down on a rough drawing, it's a good idea to tidy these up when you get back inside. The best way to do this is to draw a neat scale plan. Some people prefer to do this on graph paper, perhaps using each large square to represent one square metre (on 1cm graph paper this would be a scale of 1:100). This is fine, but be careful not to let the squares dictate your design too much – it can be tempting to stick with straight lines and angular shapes on graph paper. Another option is to draw your plan on plain paper, using a calculator to work out the scaled-down measurements and a ruler to draw these on to the paper. A scale ruler is a useful tool here, and can be bought from any good art shop.

You should draw to the largest scale that you can fit onto your paper, and might want to draw a 'close-up' plan of very detailed parts of the garden to an even larger scale. There's no need to write all your measurements onto a scale plan – this would crowd the drawing and confuse the design. Instead, you can just measure from the finished drawing and scale up.

A question of scale

The idea of large and small scale can be confusing; just think of it in terms of the size of the finished drawing. A 1:20 drawing would be much larger than a 1:100 drawing of the same thing. The following scales are commonly used because it's easy to multiply up and down in round numbers:

Large-scale				Small-scale
1:20	1:50	1:100	1:200	1:500

Creating a design

Once you're armed with an accurate scale drawing of your garden, or at least a good sketch with measurements, you're ready to start trying your ideas. Remember that your design will develop as you add different elements, so you may need to work and rework the drawing many times. An architect once told me the tool he used most often was an eraser! Don't ruin your neat scale plan by drawing straight on to it – make a few photocopies (with the copier set at 100% to avoid any change in scale) and keep one as the master.

The first stages of design can be the most daunting part of the process – just where do you begin? The thing to remember is that nothing you do on paper binds you to anything in real life. Just start putting thoughts down and keep coming back with changes and new thoughts. All you have to lose at this stage is a few sheets of paper. Even a quickly scribbled line can give you the inspiration that leads to a final idea.

A roll or pad of tracing paper can be very helpful at this stage; by laying it over a copy of your master plan you can sketch in new elements and ideas without redrawing the whole site each time you make a mistake. Switch to a new sheet of trace to try a different idea, then overlay multiple sheets to combine different concepts. When you've decided which of your ideas are working together best, simply trace them off again on to a final plan.

Tracing paper can also be laid over a photo of the existing garden, allowing you to sketch your ideas over the top. Copy any elements that you intend to keep, and you'll quickly see an 'artist's impression' taking shape. This is ideal for working out how your design will look from a given viewpoint (such as the back door, or the kitchen window). Take photos from these important viewpoints and develop a sketch for each one.

If you're finding it hard to decide where various elements of your design should go, you might try making scale drawings of each one and then cutting them out. These paper templates can be moved from place to place so that you can quickly

compare different combinations. This is also a great way to understand how movable items like patio furniture, barbecues and children's play equipment might work in different locations, and it will give you a better appreciation of just how much space these items can take up and so help you avoid building patios and decks that are too small to be used practically.

Making a model

The next step on from a two-dimensional plan, models are more time-consuming to make but give you a much more realistic perspective of any layout. Use strong card to make the back wall of the house, boundary walls and fences, existing outbuildings and so on. You can then use layers of card or paper, coloured if you like, to represent lawns, paths, paving and other flat surfaces. Trees and shrubs can be modelled using a cocktail stick for the trunk or main stem, with several concentric circles of card spaced up this to represent the foliage. A visit to a hobby or craft store will give you plenty of ideas – be as creative as you like!

Principles of design

Without wanting to turn this book into a great work on garden design, I think it's worth mentioning a few simple principles that are easy to apply but can have really striking effects, and prevent the garden from looking like a mismatched jumble of ideas. All great designs, from landscape and architecture, through cars, clothes and even music, follow rules of scale, rhythm and proportion. Far from being restrictive, even a simple grasp of these basics can give you all sorts of design inspiration:

Scale

This is a simple rule, but one that must be carefully followed. Match the dimensions within your design to those of the space available. In other words, a small garden will be dominated by a very large patio, while a tiny patio in the corner of a spacious plot will look ridiculous. This also applies to timber structures such as summer houses and pergolas, and even to statues and other ornaments.

Proportion

There are 'golden rules' of proportion that can be followed to give a pleasing sense of something just 'feeling right'. For example, a patio that is twice as long as it is wide (in other words 1:2, or a double square) will probably feel well-proportioned. Likewise a lawn that is one and a half times longer than wide (a very handy ratio of 1:1.5, or 2:3) will somehow feel comfortable to look at. This technique of doubling and halving dimensions, and sticking to ratios of 1:2 and 2:3, is also sensible from a construction point of view; materials tend to come in standard sizes, so you can reduce the time spent cutting as well as the waste left at the end.

Geometry

The human eye is drawn by regular shapes such as circles, triangles and squares. Use combinations of these and don't be afraid to rotate, overlap or interlock each with the next. Experiment on paper to find combinations that work well together within the available space.

Route

Many gardens, particularly larger ones, are designed to be walked through. If this is your aim, think about how you'll progress from one point to the next (and provide paths accordingly), then consider how you can create experiences and interest along each stage of the journey.

Formal/informal

Straight lines and regular spacing of vertical objects will make you garden feel smart and formal, which is great if you have a house to match. Curves and circles, combined with irregular planting, will give a sense of relaxed, almost accidental informality. In fact both should be carefully planned at the design stage.

Focal point

An easy way to design is to choose the element that's most important to you (often a main seating area) and design outwards from this. At all times consider how the main feature will be seen from other areas of the garden – you're aiming to draw people in.

Repetition

Using a limited palette of colours and repeating similar shapes and materials is a great way to bring a sense of uniformity to your design. Try to match the materials you use to those already in place in the surrounding garden. The same goes for shapes, colours and styles.

Low-maintenance gardens

For most of us, relaxation is the number one reason for having a garden. That may mean space to play with the kids, somewhere to throw a party for friends and family, or a spot where you can enjoy a comfy sun lounger, a glass of wine and a good book. What we don't need is a garden which takes hours of our time every week and yet, despite our best efforts, never looks 'under control'!

But you don't have to be a fanatical gardener to really enjoy the great outdoors – many of the plants and other products available in garden centres are deliberately targeted at people who don't have much time to spare – people who want minimum-effort, low-maintenance solutions to the problem of keeping a garden tidy through the year. Landscaping can really help with this; by choosing the right materials you can save yourself a great deal of effort.

Low-maintenance ideas

Paving
A patio or terrace has to be the easiest garden feature to look after. A scrub once a year and the occasional sweep is all that's required.

Decking
Timber decks are easier to install than paving, and almost as low-maintenance. A coat of preservative every three years should keep it in good shape.

Perennial shrubs
These grow for many years, and therefore don't need much attention beyond the occasional prune, and watering when young. Combine with mulching for best effect.

Natural landscaping
Create a garden that's close to nature and you can simply leave it to look after itself, besides a little weeding and watering. The style will depend on your local climate.

Mulching
A mulch is a layer of loose material, often wood chip or gravel, laid on landscaping fabric spread over bare soil. It prevents the growth of weeds, keeps the soil moist (so less watering) and looks good too.

Planning permission in the garden

One thing that may restrict your options at the design stage is planning law. While garden landscaping is less drastic than extending or converting your house, and doesn't go as far as to include extensive structures like garages, there are still aspects of it which come under the control of the planning authority. And rightly so – the height of fences and walls, and the size and position of sheds and other structures, are all controlled to avoid people over-developing their gardens and inconveniencing their neighbours. The rules can vary from one authority to the next, but there are basic laws that apply to us all. For example, garden structures up to a certain size and height are generally allowed under a system known as permitted development. There are also different rules for houses and flats.

Planning guidelines for house owners

- Fences and walls – You're unlikely to require permission to install, or to alter or improve, a fence or wall up to 2m in height, unless it borders a highway in which case the maximum height is 1m.
- Patios – There are normally no restrictions to building a patio anywhere in your back garden, although substantial related works of embanking or terracing may be an exception.

- Driveways – Hard standing in the front garden doesn't require permission if it's permeable and allows rainwater to pass through – such as porous blocks or gravel – or if it drains onto a lawn or border. Non-permeable surfaces of greater than 5m^2 require permission.
- Decking – Now classed as permitted development, provided it's not more than 30cm above the ground and covers no more than 50% of the total garden.
- Garden buildings – These are a permitted development, but you're not allowed to build structures more than one storey tall. The maximum eaves height mustn't exceed 2.5m, and overall height mustn't exceed 4m (with a dual pitched roof) or 3m (any other roof). The maximum overall height drops to 2.5m if within 2m of a boundary. You may not build in front of the house, nor build over more then 50% of the garden.
- Listed buildings – You're more likely to need planning permission for any of the above if you live in or adjacent to a listed building, or in a conservation area.

Residents of flats or maisonettes face many more restrictions, and are likely to have to apply for planning permission to erect a shed, greenhouse, wall or fence of any size, or even to build an area of hard standing such as a patio! If you're in any doubt a call to your local planning office is the best way forward. Far from being the difficult or dismissive people they're sometimes said to be, in my experience planning officers are both helpful and friendly.

TOOLS, MATERIALS AND EQUIPMENT

2

Tools, materials and equipment

Once you've created a beautiful design for your garden, or at least for the part of it you'd like to change, the next step is to make preparations for the work involved. In this chapter we will look at all the tools that might come in useful for a range of garden projects, from working the soil to building in stone and wood. We will also discuss the materials themselves, including purchasing, delivery and disposal, plus how to dress and work safely.

Safety clothing

■ Overalls
A good strong set of overalls will keep unpleasant materials away from your skin and protect your clothes. A simple set won't cost much, but if you prefer – and are prepared for them to be ruined – you can wear tough old clothes, provided they have full-length sleeves and legs.

■ Gloves
You'll need more than one pair of sturdy work gloves. The rigger style is the most versatile, and is perfect for most digging, timber and stone work. Thick rubber ones may be better when working with cement, and can give more grip with brick and stone.

■ Boots or shoes
Strong, grippy footwear is essential, especially in wet conditions. If working with heavy materials, such as paving slabs or railway sleepers, it's important to have protective toecaps.

■ Particle mask
A simple paper mask will prevent the inhalation of dust and some fumes. You'll appreciate this when you take the mask off and look at the dirt caked on the outside! For extended or hazardous jobs buy a proper respirator with replaceable filters.

■ Goggles
Stone chips and splinters, especially those thrown up by power tools, can do serious harm to unprotected eyes. A pair of simple plastic goggles will prevent this happening and will also keep the worst of airborne dust at bay.

■ Ear defenders
Only necessary if you're using loud power tools such as a plate compactor, demolition drill or angle grinder, and particularly for longer jobs.

Surveying and marking out

■ Spirit levels (long and standard)
Finding a horizontal line is an important part of many construction jobs. A long spirit level is ideal for larger projects and particularly for ground works. Smaller levels are useful for more detailed work, for example ensuring that individual paving slabs are laid flat.

■ Surveyor's tape measure
An extra-long tape for measuring greater distances, mostly useful at the planning stage. Usually either 30m or 50m long.

■ A 5m tape measure
An invaluable tool that should never be far out of reach. Avoid the budget designs; you'll use this so often it's worth spending a little more on a good-quality model.

■ Timber pegs and string
Make your own from any offcuts. Useful for marking out groundworks; simply drive the pegs into the ground and tie string between them.

■ Marker paint
An alternative to pegs and string, marker paint is simply sprayed onto the ground. It's only suitable for rough marking out, as the spray is too broad to be very precise.

■ Graph or plain paper
Use one pad for taking measurements 'in the field', then transfer this information to a neater plan when indoors. The larger the sheet of paper, the more detail you can include.

Getting equipped

'Use the right tool for the job' is an old saying, but the reason it's so familiar is that we all know it to be good advice. Some tasks can be completed in a number of different ways, but there are other occasions when we have to follow a certain method, and the tools we require will be just as specific. Not only will this make your job much easier, but there's a safety aspect to consider too. Making do with poor quality, broken or simply unsuitable tools is a drain on your concentration, a physical strain, and a likely source of all kinds of accidents. The right tool is not a luxury, it's an absolute necessity. This doesn't mean you have to spend thousands of pounds on items you'll only use once or twice – most tools are useful for many other jobs, and so represent an investment that will repay you many hundreds of times over even if you're only an occasional DIYer. Some items are undeniably more specialised, but the more expensive ones can be hired by the day.

■ Pencils
Propelling pencils are best as they don't require sharpening halfway through a survey.

■ Compass
Finding out the aspect of your plot is very important, and a compass is the best way to do this.

■ Carpenter's (or builder's) square
A large item, but folding versions are quite common and much easier to store. This is a simple way of determining if corners are square, either when surveying or when building.

Clearance and demolition

■ Loppers

A long-handled pair will give you the leverage to cut through stems and branches up to 4cm thick. Ratchet designs require less strength to use.

■ Secateurs

Vital for keeping shrubs and small trees in shape, and for cutting back very overgrown areas.

■ Pruning saw

Ideal for taking off smaller branches without harming the tree. They usually cut on the pull stroke for ease of use.

■ Bow saw

A larger saw for removing thicker branches. Be careful not to underestimate the weight of the wood you're cutting, and certainly don't stand beneath the branch.

■ Crow bar

Only required if you're lifting old paving, or demolishing unwanted garden buildings.

■ Brush-cutter or strimmer

A fast way to clear large areas of long grass or weeds. Brush-cutters have steel blades and are best for thick weeds like brambles, while strimmers have nylon cords and are better for grass.

■ Shredder

Ideal if you have lots of prunings to dispose of. Electric or petrol shredders will reduce this waste to useful chippings.

■ Demolition drill

The least labour-intensive way to break up unwanted concrete or masonry is to use one of these. Ear defenders and eye protection are a must, and you should take regular breaks from the heavy physical work.

Groundwork

■ Digging spade

A real garden workhorse, your spade should be kept clean and sharp so that it slices through the soil effectively. Don't scrimp here – a good-quality spade will be with you for a lifetime.

■ Digging fork

Used more for breaking up soil than for moving it, the tines of a garden fork are designed to be easy to push into the ground. Again, quality is worth paying for in a tool you'll use so often.

■ Shovel

Not to be confused with a spade, this has a wider head with a raised back and edges. Used for moving large quantities of loose soil, gravel or other materials.

■ Soil rake

A long handle and short, rectangular head with strong tines to level soil, sand, gravel and so on. Can also be used vertically to 'tamp-down' or compact loose materials, but don't use too much pressure or the head may bend.

■ Pickaxe

Not often used, but invaluable when you need it. Used for breaking up rock, masonry, old concrete and very compacted or dry soil.

■ Garden trowel

For the finer details and tight corners you'll often need something smaller than a spade. Also useful as a measure when making up small quantities of concrete or mortar.

■ Sledgehammer

Used both for demolition (of any unwanted masonry structures) and for construction (driving fence posts and stakes into the ground). Can also be used up-ended for compacting loose materials.

■ Plate compactor

You really don't want to be compacting the foundations of a large patio or drive using just an up-ended sledgehammer. A plate compactor is nothing more than a vibrating motor attached to a large flat plate, but it can save many hours of hard work. Drag it back and forth over crushed hardcore to get a good solid base.

■ Garden roller

Not often used these days, rollers can help flatten an uneven lawn, or in construction to compact light materials such as sand.

■ Wheelbarrow

You'll do some miles with one of these, so buy the best you can afford. A strong front wheel is essential, but both steel and plastic bodies (if robust) are good options. Apart from moving materials you can also use your barrow to mix concrete, but be sure to wash it well afterwards.

■ Mini digger

Perhaps not something to rush out and buy, mini diggers can be hired for a sensible price. They take the hard work out of digging footings, and can come with an operator if you don't fancy the driving.

Masonry tools

■ Club hammer
A smaller version of a sledgehammer, designed for use with one hand. Used for light demolition, driving in stakes, and with a bolster or chisel to cut bricks and slabs.

■ Brick hammer
A specialist tool with one blunt side to the head and a second sharper, flatter side. Used for chipping bricks into shape.

■ Bolster
A large, flat-headed chisel for cutting bricks into smaller pieces, or for making neat holes in masonry. Look for one with a sturdy hand guard.

■ Cold chisel
Used for making small, precise cuts into dry mortar, brick or stone, this chisel has a narrow, flat head.

■ Plugging chisel
Similar in appearance to a cold chisel, the plugging variety has a head tapered from one side to the other. Its purpose is to cut out old mortar; use it point-inwards to channel deeper into the mortar, point-outwards to remain shallow.

■ Mason's trowel
A large, flat, triangular trowel used for applying mortar when bricklaying. It takes a little practice to use effectively, but once mastered it works brilliantly.

■ Pointing trowel
A smaller tool for detailed work, but essentially the same design as a mason's trowel.

■ Rubber mallet
Getting slabs flat and level is very important, and a rubber mallet allows you to knock them down one corner at a time without damaging the surface.

■ Builder's line and pins
A pair of steel pins with a string line between them, useful for creating a level-guide when bricklaying. The pins are flat, and can be pushed into mortar joints.

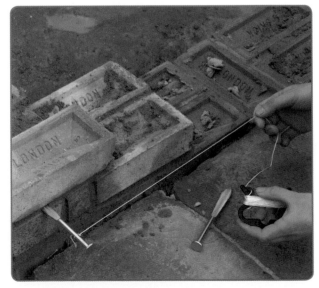

■ Bucket

For mixing small quantities of mortar, washing tools, measuring materials and a million other jobs to boot. Buy two or three, and make sure the bucket and the handle are both strongly made.

■ Spacers

For maintaining an even gap or joint between paving slabs. Make your own by sawing a length of dowel into smaller pieces; the diameter of the dowel gives you the size of the gap.

■ Angle grinder

A power tool with a rapidly spinning disc that can grind through stone and even cut neatly through sheet metal, depending on the type of disc you use. Very handy for cutting large slabs down to size.

■ Cement mixer

Can be hired, more to save you the storage space than the expense (electric versions can be found for under £100).

Power tools in the garden

Some DIY jobs can be completed quite easily using only hand tools, but there are many where power tools really come into their own. Although they're more expensive, you'll find that buying the right ones saves you many hours of hard work over the lifetime of the tool – a wise investment in my opinion. When you're working outdoors, cordless tools are by far the best option. Not only do they make it much easier to move around without worrying about a power supply, but they're also safer as they don't require cables running across the garden or an electricity supply out where the conditions may be wet and unpredictable.

First on the shopping list has to be a combination drill/driver – something you'll find yourself using on almost every project. I'd also recommend a cordless saw to take the effort out of any woodwork. Go for the best models you can afford and remember that the accessories (drill bits and saw blades) limit the performance of the tool, so don't cut corners here. You may also want to consider buying an angle grinder, circular saw, nail and/or screw gun. All of these are worth considering, depending on the type of work you anticipate doing more regularly.

Woodworking tools

■ Claw hammer
The classic hammer design, with one part of the head for driving nails and tacks, and the other for prying them out.

■ Hand saw
For cutting all types of timber. Some blades cut quickly, others neatly, so consider what you need before buying. The handle can also often be used to measure 90° and 45° angles.

■ Combination square
An adjustable guide that can be pressed against the edge of your timber to mark out any angle.

■ Bradawl
Simply a sharp metal point with a wooden handle, used for creating small starter holes so that screws can be easily driven in.

■ Screwdrivers
A good range of sizes is essential, both in flat-headed and cross-headed configurations.

Caring for tools

With one or two exceptions, building tools are usually designed to take quite a battering through their lives yet still remain functional. That said, they'll quickly degrade if you don't give them at least some basic care. One thing to watch out for is rust – metal tools left outdoors, or those thrown in a damp corner after use, will quickly lose their surface finish. This is particularly bad news for those with a cutting edge.

Get into the habit of cleaning your tools after each session, using either a stiff brush (to remove soil from digging tools) or a jet from a hose (for cement-encrusted building tools). Dry them well and put them away carefully. If you don't intend to use them for more than a few weeks, give any metal surfaces a light spray with oil.

■ Timber chisels
For cutting neat holes in timber, mostly when fitting two parts of a joint together or when installing doors and windows.

■ Cordless jigsaw
A fast, if not particularly neat, way of cutting timber. Use with a guide for long straight cuts, or freehand to create intricate curves.

Miscellaneous tools

■ Cordless drill/ screwdriver with bits
An invaluable addition to the outdoor-DIYer's toolbox. A good multi-purpose design can drill holes in masonry, metal and timber, as well as driving screws and bolts into place.

■ Stanley knife
For anything from opening packaging and keeping your pencil sharp to marking timber and cutting sheet materials.

■ Pliers
For gripping, grabbing and bending all kinds of things. A design with an inbuilt wire-cutter is particularly handy.

■ Adjustable spanners, various sizes
For tightening nuts and bolts in timber construction. Also useful when plumbing-in water features.

■ Paintbrush
For painting, of course, but also for brushing fine grit into place and simply for making things wet to aid adhesion or to reduce dust.

■ Dustpan and brush
Both for cleaning up at the end of a job and for moving loose materials into place.

■ Stiff broom
Naturally this is for sweeping, but a stiff broom in particular is also useful for scrubbing stone and timber to remove stains and algae.

■ Spring tine rake
For removing the 'thatch' of old grass and moss from turf, and for clearing fallen leaves and cut grass.

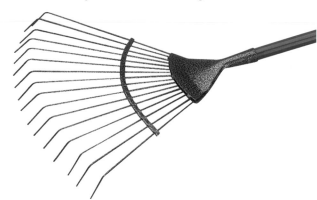

Buy or hire?

Large power tools are expensive to buy and can take up a lot of storage space when they're not in use. They're also less often used than many smaller tools, although they're often the key to a successful, less-stressful project. It's therefore often a better idea to hire some of the tools you need, perhaps for a week or just a weekend, rather than investing lots of cash with the intention of using the tools again in the future. Even if you're sure you'll use such tools more than once, hire centres are still worth investigating, as they service and maintain the tools in between jobs – saving you the trouble.

Tools most commonly hired for garden landscaping purposes are cement mixers, plate compactors and mini diggers, with power drills, angle grinders, jigsaws and other hand-held equipment also available. Ask around for prices – not just in dedicated tool-hire centres but also in builders' merchants. Some companies will offer excellent rates for a weekend, when such items are not booked out by professional builders.

Be aware when hiring that the price you pay for using the equipment is not necessarily the only cost. There will also be consumables to pay for (such as the cutting discs of an angle grinder, and very often petrol). You may also face further charges if you don't clean the tools properly before you return them – be sure to ask about this in advance, and check that you know exactly what day and time the tools must be returned.

Getting rid of waste

One of the most labour-intensive elements of a garden landscaping project can often be removing the stuff you don't want – be it soil, plant matter or general garden rubbish. You should plan for this before your project gets under way.

For small jobs you may be able to remove all the waste materials yourself, particularly if you have access to a car. Civic amenity sites (often called 'the tip') have special collection points for timber, soil, green waste, rubble and much more. This is quite a green option because all the materials will be properly recycled, but it does mean you have to get the stuff there. There are often small local firms who will collect waste for you, but you should check that they're licensed to dispose of it before you agree to anything. Too many waste-filled vans are unloaded into some poor farmer's field along a quiet country road!

Skip hire

Hiring a skip is an excellent way to reduce the effort involved in clearing a plot, in particular transporting excavated soil. Skips come in a wide range of sizes, often referred to in the UK by the yard. There are two-yard, four-yard, six-yard, right up to twelve-yard skips and beyond, the larger ones being more suited to house clearances and the like. In fact these names refer to the volume of the skip – hence two, four and six *cubic* yards. As long as you know this, you can work out how much waste a skip will hold. A two-yard skip, sometimes called a mini-skip, is really quite small. For basic garden jobs you'll be looking at a four-yard model, and for more extensive work you'll need a six- or eight-yarder. Although the cubic yard is a rather old-fashioned unit of measurement, it's easy to convert this to metres. Two cubic yards are about equal to 1.5 cubic metres.

To work out the volume of soil you'll excavate, perhaps for a patio, multiply the width of the excavation by the length. Multiply the result by the depth (see Chapter 3 for more on this) and you have the volume. Make sure each measurement is in metres and your result will be in cubic metres. However, soil increases in volume by as much as 100% when it's broken up, so to be on the safe side you should double the volume before you book your skip. As an example, an excavation measuring 4m long 2.5m wide by 0.25m deep will require $2.5m^3$ of soil to be removed, which will roughly double in size to $5m^3$ as it's dug up. This will overfill a six-yard skip (which holds $4.5m^3$), or leave you room in an eight-yarder (which holds $6m^3$) for the paving offcuts, packaging and other waste. It's always worth booking the slightly bigger skip in this case.

Success with skips

There are plenty of cowboys in the skip hire business, so ask around before you book one. Word of mouth is the only way you can know who's reliable – a local firm with a long history of satisfied customers is the best bet.

Talk to the hire company about your requirements, both in terms of the skip itself and the drop-off point. Skip wagon drivers are usually among the best on the road and will do their utmost to drop where you want them too, but give them as much info as possible before they arrive.

Stick to the skip company's rules about how much your skip can hold, and what can go in it. Drivers are legally required to refuse to move an overfilled skip, or one containing the wrong kind of waste.

Skips left on a public highway (necessary if you don't have a drive or front garden) require a permit from your local council. These vary wildly from one council to the next, from free permits issued the same day to those costing the best part of £100 and taking two weeks to arrange. Some skip companies will arrange this for you, others will ask you to approach the council direct.

If your skip can be accessed by the public, aim to fill it and have it removed quickly. It doesn't take long for unscrupulous passers-by to fill your skip for you!

Choosing your materials

What materials you use will affect the way you design your garden, as well as how you use it and how it needs to be maintained. As a general rule, the more effort it takes to install something, the longer it will last and the less maintenance will be required. That means if you want a really low-maintenance garden you need to put in lots of ground work. For example, stone and concrete paving take a major investment of time and physical effort, but will last for 20 years or more with just the occasional weeding. Timber takes less time to install, but will last 10 to 15 years and needs more regular attention. Loose aggregates such as gravel, as well as grass and plants, will increase your involvement still further, so do consider how much time you can spare before you start.

It's a good idea to match any new textures, colours and styles to those already in place – for example, if your house is a country cottage you might consider using old bricks for paths, and roughly-finished natural stone for a seating area. A more modern house might suit a garden with plenty of smart timber (think decking and balustrading) and perhaps a more regular reconstituted-stone paved area. Good designs should look like they've always been there, or at least were intended from the day the garden was created.

Timber

The basic techniques of cutting, drilling and shaping timber are easy to pick up, and will be invaluable throughout your DIY life. One of the easiest and most forgiving of materials to work with, timber is also a very cost-effective alternative to stone if you're looking to create a durable seating area. Apart from decking, timber is useful in other areas of garden building. Sheds, fencing, arbours, trellises and much more are all best approached with timber construction in mind, and the finished project will age and weather attractively to blend into your scheme.

An important idea to master when using timber is that of working to a grid. In other words, structural elements such as upright posts and horizontal beams and joists should be spaced evenly rather than randomly. What's more, your grid should match the sizes of the timber you're working with – so that sheet materials and cladding don't have to be cut down any more than is necessary. For example, if the cladding you intend to use comes in planks 1.2m long, why not make your shed 1.2m or 2.4m wide? If you want something in between, 1.8m requires only one cut every second row of planks, whereas any other dimension would require twice that many cuts and leave you with a big pile of wasted timber.

Stone, brick and concrete

Although it isn't the easiest material to cut or shape, stone (and the various reconstituted products that are now available) doesn't require any really advanced skill to use unless your project is complicated. As with timber, it's wise to bear in mind the sizes of your materials before you finalise your design. If you're using paving slabs of a set size, or of a range of set sizes, it's worth planning on paper exactly how they'll be laid out, bearing in mind that you'll need to leave even gaps between them. For many years there has been a

great deal of snobbery associated with natural stone, but reconstituted products are now almost impossible to fault, and are often a much greener option because they make use of a waste product (the dust and chippings from other stone products). They're also more regular in their shape and appearance than natural stone, which may be a plus or a minus point depending on your requirements.

Concrete is magical stuff that has many thousands of uses, but in a garden setting it's generally employed as a malleable base material, poured into excavated footings, levelled and left to go hard. Concrete is made up from cement, aggregate (commonly sharp sand and coarse gravel) and water, sometimes with a few chemical additives thrown in to adjust its physical qualities. The exact mixture depends on the end use, and we'll talk more about that in Chapter 3.

Plants and soil

Plants are the most difficult aspect of garden design to get exactly right – they have their own ideas about where they should grow, and how fast they should get there. This, of course, is one of the main challenges of gardening –

predicting and influencing this growth to get a pleasing result. The plants you choose may be an eclectic mix of whatever takes your fancy in the garden centre, or perhaps a tightly-controlled group of complementary species and styles. Either way, shopping for them is great fun! Be sure to choose those that will be happy in your garden – consider your aspect and exposure (see Chapter 1) as well as your soil type. It's hard work growing plants that aren't happy in their location.

Some garden makeovers require soil to be moved for reasons other than construction – perhaps you want to create a bank or hollow, or flatten or terrace an uneven plot. Large quantities of soil can take a major effort to move, so allow plenty of time for this and consider calling in help where it's available. Turf is also a surprisingly heavy material, particularly if it's been kept well watered (which it will have been if you buy from a good supplier). Keeping grass in good condition is an art form, and if the perfect green sward matters to you then you'll need to put in lots of time and effort. That said, a lawn is one of the most versatile and useful parts of a garden.

Gravel and loose aggregates

Loose materials such as gravel, wood chip, bark and slate chippings all have their own unique character, as well as some general advantages and disadvantages. They're a wonderfully easy way to cover ground, particularly in

awkwardly shaped corners, and if used on top of a water-permeable, weed-excluding membrane (sometimes sold as landscaping fabric) they can be a great way of preventing weed growth between your plants. They're also a very economical option, ideal for gardeners on a budget.

Drawbacks include the mobility of the material – weather, children and pets can spread your neatly-raked aggregates all over a patio or lawn (and thus up into your lawnmower). That they're really only suited to flat or very gently sloped gardens. They can also become a toilet area for the local cats, particularly if you opt for a finer grade. A beautiful Zen garden loses much of its appeal when treated as a giant litter tray.

Reclaimed materials

If you don't mind a few imperfections or irregularities, using second-hand, salvaged or otherwise reclaimed materials can be a very satisfying option. Look up your local architectural salvage or reclaim yards and pay them each a visit – they're a great source of inspiration and you may find yourself losing hours among their diverse contents. Timber of all shapes and sizes, bricks, stone and other building materials are all widely available, as are statues and garden ornaments. You may even find something unusual – a Doric column or an old church window – around which you can create a whole new design. Recycling in this way is very environmentally conscious, as not only are you stopping something from going to a landfill site but you're also opting-out of the consumption of new resources. What's more it can be a great way to save money, though you may be shocked at the price of some of the more fashionable materials.

Working safely

It's worth taking your time to do any job safely, no matter how fit or capable you are, as a simple mistake can be very dangerous when you're dealing with power tools and garden machinery.

After you're kitted out with the appropriate safety clothing, perhaps the most general rule of thumb is not to push yourself too hard. By this I mean don't try to lift too much, don't try to work for too long, and most importantly (at least in my experience) don't try to go too fast! The few times I've injured myself in the course of a DIY project have all been when I've been rushing to get a job finished before the light fails, or before I have to dash off somewhere else. It's a false economy, of course, because it takes me twice as long to get anything done when I have a bandaged hand or a sore back.

Other important rules are to keep your working area as clean and tidy as you can; not to let people or pets into the working area without precautions; always to read the instructions supplied with tools and materials; and not to work alone when carrying out any task that involves potential dangers.

Hazards to be aware of include trailing wires from power tools (always try to buy cordless options), heavy weights, uneven and slippery surfaces, and even chemicals – cement, for example, can be quite nasty stuff if you get it on bare skin.

GARDEN LANDSCAPING

HARD LANDSCAPING

3

Hard Landscaping

A perfect way to cut your list of weekend gardening chores is to use paving and decking to create versatile and robust areas of 'hard landscaping' – it's easy to look after and instantly expands the potential of your garden. These areas are easy and comfortable to walk and relax on, simple to keep clean and looking good, and can be used in all weathers without the risk of bringing dirt and mud into the house. They're the perfect intermediary zone between the indoor environment of the house and the rest of the garden, and are often built adjacent to kitchen or patio doors.

Hard landscaping also covers walls and steps, both of which are important in many sloping garden designs. While these are more challenging proposals they're a valuable method of creating vertical interest, as well as being a practical necessity in some situations. In this chapter we'll look at the realities of each of these projects, and discuss the details of the construction processes.

When it comes to hard landscaping it's important to take your time at the planning stage, since these alterations are very difficult to remove or adjust once

they're in place. Consider what lies beneath the proposed site of new paving – will you need access to any services that run through the garden? Also give some thought to how you'll bring large tools and materials to the site – must they come through the house, or is there a less intrusive point of access?

Paths

Well-designed paths, linking the most regularly used parts of the garden, cut down on muddy footprints inside the house and make jobs like taking out the rubbish or picking a few home-grown herbs much more pleasant. They can be thought of as structural elements – once in place they influence what else you can do around them – so think well about where and how you'll build them. The width of a path is clearly very important; a major route along which people will pass each other or walk side by side should be 1.5m wide at least. This will allow the plants in adjacent borders to intrude slightly without obstructing, but don't let them get too out of control. If you require wheelchair access you should allow a little more width. Subsidiary paths, intended more for quick access by one person, can be as narrow as 0.9m, but this would mean that several people travelling down them together would have to walk in single file.

What material you use to surface your paths depends on the style of your garden and the purpose of the path. A grand walkway straight up the middle of a large and formal design would look great paved with wide stone slabs, probably laid to a very regular pattern. A winding track that explores the hidden depths of a private country garden would look much better completed in old brick, which would weather and age beautifully. The two materials would require different foundations, as we'll discuss later, but there are elements of the design process that apply to all types and styles of path.

Desire lines

It's pretty obvious why most of us choose the shortest route between two points when we need to get somewhere: it's the most direct and time-efficient option, and it gets us

where we want to be. Any deviations from this route will feel like a chore, which is precisely why you so often see tracks worn into the grass on roadside verges close to pedestrian crossings – people simply can't be bothered to walk along two sides of a verge when the diagonal route across the grass is more direct. These tracks are the physical manifestation of something designers refer to as 'desire lines', essentially the ideal paths people create in their minds to reach their objective. These will also exist in your garden and it's very important to cater for them if you want people to stick to the paths you're going to build.

Imagine a garden with a beautiful central lawn, with the house on one side and a sunny patio on the other. If the path you build from house to patio takes a circuitous route, from the back door around the edge of the garden to one side of the patio, it will probably be used only rarely. Instead you'll find that people walk straight across the lawn, and a worn strip of grass will develop if the patio is used frequently. In other words, plan with desire lines in mind and your paths will be a useful and successful addition to the garden.

Patios

A well-designed area of paving is often the number one item on a gardener's wish list. It allows for a much longer season of use than a lawn and involves considerably less maintenance. It's also probably the most expensive alteration you'll make to your plot and it's therefore important to do it right.

The size of any paved area is, of course, limited by the size of the garden. However, many patios are built too small to be aesthetically appropriate to the house. A good way to determine what will look right is to measure the height of the adjacent house walls (up to the eaves), then transfer this horizontally on to the ground, measuring from the house wall outwards. Of course, we don't all have the budget to fulfil all our design dreams, but a patio built too small to be practical, simply to save money, is very much a false economy. If you can't afford to build something that will work, keep saving until you can.

When it comes to choosing your surface material, many of the same rules apply as for paths. The area in question will be larger, of course, so it may be more appropriate to use larger paving slabs. That said, a patio surfaced with bricks will be very effective too.

Consider the view

One thing to think about when positioning a patio is what you'll see when you sit on it. Ideally you should have pleasant views across the garden, perhaps with unobstructed sight lines to key features like ponds or

beds of ornamental plants. If you're lucky you might be able to take advantage of views further afield, across the neighbouring countryside. What you want to avoid is a view of bin stores, tatty garden sheds or the neighbours' washing line. An enclosed patio, with views of nothing more than four brick walls, can often work well if you furnish and plant it cleverly; you're simply turning the attention inwards to a more private environment.

Edging paths and patios

It's perfectly possible to use concrete or stone slabs to build a paved area with edges that simply butt-up against the surrounding turf or borders. Provided you measure the levels properly during construction, so that the upper surface of the paving is neither lower than its surroundings (leading to soil creeping on to the paving) nor higher (exposing unsightly edges), the transition between materials will look fine. However, for a slightly more professional look you might consider adding some form of edging.

Many paving companies supply strips or blocks of edging that are matched perfectly to their ranges of paving materials, but you also have the option of creating a contrast between the two. For example, a softly-coloured limestone patio or path edged with a row of old red bricks will look very appealing.

The edging material can be flush with the paving on one side and the surrounding turf or soil on the other – this gives a purely visual boundary and the rule about getting the levels right still applies. There are also edging products that stand proud of the ground level, creating a low physical barrier as well as a visual one. These are ideal if you want to use loose aggregates (such as gravel or chipped bark) adjacent to the paving, as they'll stop the wind and rain from blurring the edges. All types of edging tend to look attractive when plants are used to soften them; simply allow spreading and creeping plants to colonise the boundaries.

It's possible to add edging materials to an existing patio or path, especially if the earlier foundations were neatly built. You can also install edging as you lay the paving – just allow for the thickness when marking out your required excavations. Some types of paving require a solid edging material to hold them in place, for example blocks, brick and setts laid without mortar into a bed of sand. Without a firm edge, ideally of brick or stone laid on to a bed of concrete, the pavers will quickly start to migrate sideways.

Ideas for edging

■ Brick
A nice contrast can be achieved between brick edging and stone paving. The bricks can be laid flat or on their ends. A popular trick is to set them at a 45° angle, giving a saw-toothed effect.

■ Slate
A stylish look can be achieved with slates on edge; but be aware that they break easily, so you may need to lay several together to get a stronger result.

■ Timber
Thick boards, if correctly treated to resist rot, can be used to give a rustic look. Railway sleepers can also be used and will double-up as low seats for entertaining or for working in the border.

■ Wood
Rather than sawn timber, short logs can make a very effective border to a patio, particularly in a woodland garden. They can be stood on end and set into the ground.

■ Stone
The same material used for your paving can, of course, be stood on edge, although it may be necessary to cut the slabs to size. For a less regular appearance, pebbles or rocks can also be set into a bed of wet concrete.

Foundations for paving

In order for them to remain solid, static and free of cracks and fissures, all of your paving projects must be built on top of an appropriate foundation. Exactly what is appropriate depends on the type of surface you want to finish with, how much traffic that surface is likely to carry now and in the future, and the physical properties of the ground you're building on. Obviously a driveway or large, well-used patio needs to be supported by a more substantial (ie thicker) foundation than a simple footpath to a seat at the end of the garden. Likewise if you're building on very firm ground with no history of movement you can be less cautious than if your site is in some way unstable.

The paving material itself affects your choice of foundation – large stone or concrete slabs may crack if they move, so they're usually laid on a base of mortar. In contrast, bricks and setts are able to give slightly under pressure, and therefore are bedded tightly into compacted sand with very fine sand brushed into the joints between them. This last difference gives us two distinct methods of construction, known as rigid and flexible.

There are a few other terms worth knowing when talking about foundations. The first is that they're often also referred to

as footings or groundworks, and all three terms are variously used to describe both the excavations themselves (ie the holes before they're filled) and the finished solid structure. The term 'base' is usually used to describe the sand or mortar layer, directly on top of which the paving is laid. 'Sub-base' in turn is the layer of crushed, compacted material which commonly forms the lowest layer of a foundation.

Paving and your damp-proof course

Modern buildings are almost always built with a damp-proof course (DPC), which runs all around the external walls and prevents water from soaking up into the structure from the surrounding ground. It's a crucial part of how we keep our homes dry and comfortable, so you don't want to mess it up. Usually the DPC is around 15cm above the external ground level, so this is the minimum distance (from the top surface of paving to the DPC) that you should aim for. If the passage of time has led to a build-up of soil against the house walls, you'll need to remove more soil than would otherwise be necessary to create a foundation of the correct depth.

In older buildings, some of which may have a less than effective DPC or possibly none at all, you should be especially careful not to interrupt the natural drainage of the land around the foundations. Such venerable structures are often designed to 'breathe' through the porosity of their walls and structural elements, which means any obstruction too close to these surfaces might cause a build-up of condensation and therefore rot. It's best in this case not to build right up against the building, but instead to leave a border of soil or perhaps a loose aggregate such as gravel. It might be worth your while investigating how

the existing ground level compares to the lower part of the building walls – if it has become too high with time, remove some of the earth to prevent problems with damp. A surveyor who specialises in older buildings will give full advice if required.

Further to getting the level of your paving right, you should always make sure it slopes fractionally away from the house and other buildings so that rainwater drains in a safe direction. We'll discuss how to do this later in this chapter under the heading *Creating a fall*.

Levelling a sloping site

Building on flat ground is one thing, but what if your plot slopes? Other than a slight fall for drainage, paving should be laid flat and level, so any variation from the horizontal must be corrected before you start building. One way to do this is to cut into the ground at the higher end of the slope, then remove soil to make a flat area. This is often necessary if the garden slopes up from the house, so you step from the house on to a patio, then cross the patio and step up to the rest of the garden. You'll need some form of retaining wall to hold back the cut face of the soil beyond the paving, and the scale and construction of this wall will depend on its necessary height. A small change in level may be fine edged with one or two railway sleepers, while something greater will require a strong masonry wall. Drainage is also important – you must allow water to escape from behind the wall or the build-up of pressure could push it over.

A second option is to build a retaining wall above ground level at the bottom end of the slope, then infill behind it and build on top of the infill. This might be the best option if the slope falls away from the wall of the house. You'll need to find plenty of infill material, and to make sure it's thoroughly compacted before you build on top of it. Whether you cut into the ground, or build up on top of it, you'll probably also need to consider adding steps to give access upwards or downwards to the rest of the garden.

A third option, and perhaps the most economical in terms of both materials and energy, is to part-excavate the top end of the slope and to use the excavated soil to build up the lower part. This may involve building retaining walls at both ends, but the scale and strength of these will be much easier to manage. This is also a good way to terrace a steeply sloping garden from one end to the other, whether or not the aim is to pave those terraces.

Anatomy of a foundation

The lowest layer of your foundation will often be composed of crushed brick and concrete. It's commonly described as hardcore, and this is the term used throughout this book. If you buy hardcore from an aggregates supplier or builders' yard you should ask if it's suitable for laying a base for paving. Too many large lumps, or bits of building waste such as timber offcuts, will make the laying process more difficult, as well as degrading the final strength of your construction.

You may also be offered something called 'type one', which is a prescribed mix of solids (no larger than 37.5mm) and fines (sand and masonry dust) and is designed to leave no large voids when compacted. This is certainly a viable material for your foundation. Both hardcore and type one require compaction before anything is laid on top of them.

If your ground is unstable (for example if it has been previously excavated or has a history of movement) or if your paving will carry heavy traffic (for example a driveway) then you may want to top the hardcore with a layer of solid concrete. This makes a very strong base on which you can work. If you decide this is a good idea, you should gently rake sharp sand over the hardcore to fill any gaps in the surface. This will save on your concrete bill, as well as ensuring a stronger end result (with fewer air gaps that may eventually settle). The concrete itself is a mixture of sand, cement and water. The precise proportions depend on the properties required, but a good strong foundation mix would be one part cement, 2.5 parts sharp sand and 3.5 parts coarse aggregate (such as 20mm gravel). You can buy mixes of sand and gravel called all-in ballast, and if you prefer to work this way you would use one part cement to five parts all-in ballast.

Large paving elements (such as slabs) require a bed of mortar to hold them in place. This will be laid directly on top of the blinded hardcore (or the concrete, if you're using it)

with the pavers laid on top while the mortar is still wet. If you intend to build a flexible foundation, you'll replace the mortar layer with one made of sharp sand. This is a coarse, cheap sand which is easiest to use when slightly damp. It saves you the trouble of using a blinding layer (as it performs this purpose itself) but must be compacted in the same way as hardcore.

Foundation depths

Surface	Hardcore	Blinding	Concrete	Mortar	Sharp sand	Total*
Quick and simple path for light foot traffic	50mm**	No	No	No	50mm	50–100mm
Path for heavy use or patio on firm ground:						
slabs	100mm	Yes	No	50mm	No	150mm
setts/bricks	100mm	No	No	No	50mm	150mm
Patio on unstable ground, slab-paved driveway	100mm	Yes	75mm	50mm	No	225mm
Block or brick-paved patio	100mm	No	No	No	50mm	150mm
Block or brick-paved drive	100mm	Yes	75mm	No	50mm	225mm
Heavy-duty paved drive (for larger vehicles)	150mm	Yes	100mm	50mm	No	300mm

*Without paving   **Optional

Working out what you need

Your paving materials should be easy to order by area – indeed, some companies offer patio kits to create popular sizes and designs. As foundations are made up of successive layers of material, however, there's a little more working out to do before you order the constituent parts.

If you calculate the total area of your paving in square metres it would be nice if you could stick to metres throughout the calculations, but unfortunately most companies supply sand and hardcore by the tonne – so how far will a tonne of each go? Both hardcore and sharp sand have about the same volume-to-weight ratio, which means the coverage of both will also be about the same. Roughly speaking, one tonne of hardcore will cover 5m^2 when compacted to 100mm, and 3.5m^2 if compacted to 150mm. A tonne of sand will cover around 10m^2 at a thickness of 50mm.

Concrete can be bought ready-mixed, which is slightly more expensive but much easier than mixing your own. Suppliers often offer ready-mix by the cubic metre, which makes working out your required quantities easy. A cubic metre of concrete will cover 20m^2 at a thickness of 50mm. Of course, ready-mixed concrete is all delivered in one go, and needs to be used before it sets. For smaller projects you'd be best advised to buy the cement, sand and gravel and mix up your own concrete as you need it.

To calculate the quantities required for a concrete suitable for foundations (with a cement/sand/gravel ratio of 1:2.5:3.5),

work out the volume of concrete in cubic metres and multiply this by 320, 750 and 1,050 to get the approximate required weights of cement, sharp sand and gravel in kilograms. For example, if your patio measures 2m by 3m then its area is 6m^2. A 50mm layer of concrete would have a total volume of 0.3m^3, so that's 96kg of cement, 225kg of sharp sand and 315kg of gravel – so it's worth having that lot delivered! A third option is to buy bags of ready-mixed or 'all-in' concrete; essentially a mixture of cement and ballast to which you just add water. This saves a little time and is a good idea if you lack confidence when it comes to calculating quantities, but it can work out considerably more expensive.

Mixing concrete

While you can have ready-mixed concrete delivered, it's more cost effective to make up your own. This is especially true if you only need a small amount, when the effort of mixing is much less demanding. You can either use a rotary concrete mixer or combine the ingredients manually. The former is much less work, and electric mixers can be bought for under £200 or hired for a weekend for less than £20. All you do is measure the cement, sand and gravel, then add them to the drum with a little water. Leave to mix for a few minutes, then very slowly – and with the drum still rotating – add more water until the mix reaches the right consistency. Mixers can be tipped up (turn off the rotation first!) to empty the wet concrete into a wheelbarrow or directly on to the ground.

Mixing concrete by hand can make a real mess of the garden if you aren't careful. One option is to mix in an old wheelbarrow, which can be washed out afterwards. Another is to lay an old board on the ground and mix on top of that. After you've finished be sure to thoroughly wash buckets, barrow, spade or shovel and all laying tools, such as trowels. If the mix hardens on them they may well be ruined.

the cement rather than just dumping it in one place, and that way you should avoid forming lumps.

Keeping cement dry

As it reacts chemically with water, your supply of 'raw' cement should be kept dry until you're ready to use it. If you don't have storage space in a shed or garage, place the bags on an old palette, or planks raised up on bricks, and cover them with a plastic sheet. Leftover half-bags don't last indefinitely – perhaps only a month or so.

Concrete troubleshooter

It can take a little practice to get the mix of ingredients just right when making concrete. If you get them slightly out of proportion (particularly with regard to the amount of water), or if you haven't laid the mix properly, you may notice defects in the surface as it begins to set.

Act fast if you notice any of the following problems, and you should be able to rescue the situation.

Dimples or dips in the surface suggest air gaps underneath, into which the wet mix has settled. Add more wet concrete to fill the holes, tamp down gently until the level is correct, and smooth the surface.

A tendency for the surface to break up as you level it suggests the mix is too dry. Add a sprinkling of cement dust over the surface and spray lightly with water, before you try levelling again.

If you notice liquid pooling on top of the concrete you've probably been trowelling the mixture too much. Use the edge of your trowel to make slices in the mixture, then smooth out again immediately.

Getting the mix right

The most difficult aspect of mixing concrete is working out how much water to add. Bags of sand and gravel will both contain some water, but there's no practical way of working out how much. This means you have to judge by eye how much extra water you should add. The best way to test is to chop through your mix with a spade or trowel to form peaks or ridges. If the mix is still too dry the ridges will quickly crumble, so you'll need to add a little more water. If they're too wet they'll flop, and water may gather in the hollows. It's easy to make the mix too wet if you lack experience, but you can solve the problem by adding a handful of dry cement and working it in roughly. Make sure you sprinkle

Mixing concrete by hand

1 Measure out your sand and gravel on to the mixing area first, then measure and add the cement. Remember you're working by volume, not weight, so a foundation mix concrete will use 3.5 measures of gravel, 2.5 of sand and one of cement. What you use as a measure depends on how much you need – a bucket or shovelful (if you have a good eye) is often ideal.

2 Turn the ingredients into each other using a spade (or trowel for very small amounts). You want them well mixed, until the colour is even throughout. When combining large quantities of the ingredients it can be tricky to get the mix even all the way to the bottom, so work in smaller batches at first. This is hard going – you'll soon see why the concrete mixer was invented!

3 Make a heap of the dry ingredients, then form a crater in the top so the whole thing resembles a volcano. Pour some water into the crater (a watering can is a good way to do this accurately), taking care not to splash it over the edges. Don't add too much at first – remember that you can always add more later, but it's impossible to take any away!

4 Slowly shovel the dry mixture from the edge of the heap into the centre, until the water disappears. Then form a new crater in the middle and repeat. As the mixture starts to combine, add water in smaller amounts and make sure all of the dry ingredients are brought inwards from the edges. Continue until you achieve the correct consistency, described on page 48.

Initial excavation of foundations

1 Measure up and mark out your foundations using timber pegs linked together with taut lengths of string. Work to the exact outer limits of your paving, allowing for the thickness of any edging materials. Check with a tape measure that the dimensions are correct in every direction, and use a builder's square to ensure that any corners are exactly at right angles.

2 If you are removing turf, lift it using a spade and set it to one side. The easiest way to lift turf is to cut downwards to create one short strip at a time, then slide the spade under one end and slice horizontally along the strip about 50mm below the surface.

3 Starting from the edges and working inwards, remove the rest of the topsoil to the required depth of your foundations. The soil should be disposed of as you work, moving it away using a wheelbarrow and dumping it into a skip or spreading it elsewhere in the garden.

4 When all the soil is removed make the bottom of the excavation roughly level with a soil rake. Double check that the depth is correct right across the excavation, using a long straight board to span the width if required.

Compacting

The materials used in the construction of a foundation, particularly in the hardcore level, are by no means uniform in size and shape. As a result you must make sure they're thoroughly bedded down before you spread the next layer over the top. If you don't do this the foundation could move and settle over time, which will have disastrous effects on the upper surface of your paving. A plate compactor is the best tool for the job – you simply run it over the foundation (at least half a dozen times for each layer) and it vibrates the material into a settled state.

Using marker posts

With the final appearance and strength of your paving depending so much on the quality of the foundations, it's obviously important to have the right materials in the right place. But how do you ensure each layer is the correct thickness? The answer is to use marker posts, with lines drawn around them to act as 'levels' for each successive part of the build. With these posts driven into the base of your foundation at regular intervals (1m or 1.5m is ideal) you're never far from an accurate depth gauge.

Making marker posts

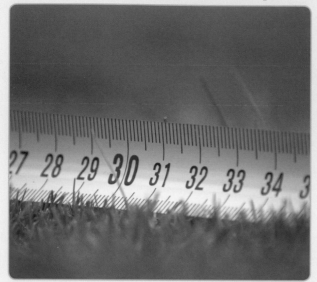

1 You can work with marker posts positioned at whatever intervals you like, but 1m and 1.5m are practical spacings. Work out how many posts you need by multiplying the number required along the length of your paving by that required across the width.

2 Cut your posts from strong timber in lengths of around 500mm – enough to be driven firmly into the soil while still leaving enough showing to mark up the depth of the paving. The timber should be thick enough to withstand heavy hammer blows – around 50mm square is fine.

3 To make the posts easier to drive into place, cut the base of each one into a point with a saw. An electric jigsaw (or a circular table-saw, if you have one) will make this much easier.

4 Now you're ready to mark the posts with your levels – a permanent marker is ideal for this. Starting at the top, measure and mark a line right around each post to show the total depth of the paving material (including the thickness of the mortar if required). Work down the posts marking each successive layer of material, according to the type of foundation you need to build.

Creating a fall

While a well-built area of paving should feel flat and level, in fact there needs to be a slight slope to the surface in order to allow rainwater to drain away properly. Without this your path or patio will quickly flood in wet weather. It's not difficult to build this slope (properly known as a 'fall') into your paving, but you must plan for it and adjust the construction of the foundations slightly.

In which direction your paving falls depends on what borders it. Water should always be directed away from house walls, sheds and other built structures. Flower beds are a suitable destination for rainwater from garden patios, while areas of lawn can absorb a limited amount of run-off from paths and smaller patios. Larger areas of paving may need to have a sunken drain constructed to carry the water into a soakaway (essentially a deep pit filled with compacted gravel). You should not direct water on to a neighbour's land.

The required fall will depend on the area of your paving; the bigger the area, the more rain will fall on it and the quicker you need to move that rain off. A typical footpath will therefore require a fall of just 1 in 80 across its width (so a drop of 12.5mm across a metre-wide path). A standard garden patio will require slightly more, perhaps 1 in 60 (a 17mm drop per 1m of width). A larger patio or driveway will require still more, up to 1 in 40 (25mm per metre).

To accurately adjust your marker posts so that they're each at the correct level to create your desired fall, simply saw a

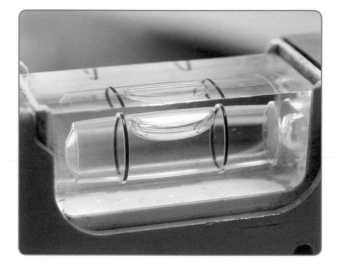

block of wood (known as a shim) to the exact thickness of the fall required between the posts. If your posts are driven in at 1m intervals, the shim should therefore be 12.5, 17 or 25mm thick depending on the slope required. If your posts are more widely spaced, multiply these thicknesses accordingly (for example, with posts 1.5m apart you'd multiply the shim thickness by 1.5).

Working from the highest side of your paving, place one end of a long spirit level on the first post. Place the other end of the spirit level on the next post, with the shim underneath. Then simply knock the second post deeper with a club hammer until the spirit level is exactly horizontal. Continue working across the excavation, knocking each post deeper in the same way.

Building rigid foundations

1 Drive your marker posts into the base of your excavation at regular intervals, until the bottom marker line of each is level with the soil. Then work across the site in the direction of the required fall, knocking each posts slightly deeper as described on page 53.

2 Use a spade, rake and trowel as necessary to adjust the soil to the correct fall, revealing the bottom line of each marker post in turn. When the fall is even from one side to the next, compact the soil thoroughly with a plate compactor or an upended sledgehammer.

3 Now add the first layer of material to the foundation – the hardcore or type 1. Spread this out evenly, without disturbing the marker posts, to the correct depth (see page 52). Compact the hardcore to settle it in place, and if this causes the level to drop add a little more material and compact again.

4 To fill air gaps in the sub-base – both to reduce future movement and to save on the amount of concrete required – you should now rake a thin layer of sharp sand over the surface. Known as 'blinding', this doesn't add significantly to the thickness of the foundation.

Further steps to be taken if an extra-strong sub-base is required:

5 A strengthening layer of concrete can be added on top of your hardcore. As this is a semi-liquid material you must contain the edges of the foundation or they'll become messy. Stout pegs and old timber boards at least 25mm thick make a good temporary boundary.

6 Don't try to mix too much concrete at once, or you'll find yourself racing the clock to get it in place before it sets. Work from one corner of the foundation outwards, and make sure you won't be cut off from the house or your tools and materials when you finish.

7 Spread the concrete evenly with a trowel, then tamp down, compressing the concrete to the correct line on the marker posts using a long straight piece of timber. Do this with one load of concrete at a time until the entire foundation is covered to the correct depth.

8 Your fresh concrete will quickly start to dry, but leave it for seven days before you build on top. In the meantime you should protect it from the weather with a layer of plastic, and from pets and people with barriers, signs and/or vigilance as appropriate.

Building flexible foundations

1 Carry out steps one to four of Step-by-Step on page 54, and steps five to eight on page 55 if an extra-strong sub-base is required, just as if you were building a rigid foundation.

2 Instead of mortar, flexible foundations have a layer of sharp sand. This is a rather mobile material and should be held in place at the edges of the foundation with an edging material set in a narrow strip of concrete, or timber boards held in place with pegs. If you set the boards deeply enough you can leave them in place and cover the tops with turf.

3 Spread the sharp sand to the correct level with a soil rake, using the lines on your marker posts as a guide. Run over the sand several times with a plate compactor – it will settle most effectively when slightly damp.

4 You can proceed with laying your paving straight away, as the sand doesn't need to dry out. If you don't wish to do this make sure the sand is protected from people, pets and weather or it will quickly lose its compaction (although it's a fairly straightforward job to repair this).

Problems with the weather?

There's no way we can ever assume we'll have the most comfortable, practical weather to work in, at least not for longer than a few hours at a time. Hot or dry spells, heavy rain and frost can all damage your foundations, and in particular any concrete you're using, but there are ways of dealing with each issue.

On a sunny day you may find that concrete dries out and sets too quickly, which can cause it to crack. This could be disastrous, as it might then no longer have the strength required to carry your paving. So avoid pouring concrete in the hottest part of the day, and consider covering the fresh slab with wet sacking, or shading it with a temporary gazebo or tarpaulin.

Rain has the potential to wash sand or concrete away (which isn't good for the health of the surrounding garden) and to make the remaining mix of concrete too wet. A simple polythene cover, held down securely with a few bricks, is the answer.

If a frost is forecast while your concrete is setting, cover it with polythene as for protection from rain. On top of this spread a 50mm layer of sand or spare soil to act as an insulating blanket. Bubble wrap, cardboard or even an old duvet could be used to protect smaller areas.

Saving your lawn

Repeated trips back and forth across your lawn, with a wheelbarrow filled with heavy soil, will quickly ruin the grass. If you must travel this way it's a good idea to lay a temporary path across the turf so that the weight of the traffic is spread out. There are special roll-out plastic paths available (they look a bit like caterpillar tracks), which are great if you need to use them often, but a much cheaper alternative is to use a few old timber planks laid end to end.

Joints in paving

Patios made from stone or concrete slabs can be laid without gaps between the slabs (known as butt-jointing), or with small gaps in between filled with dry sand, or pointed with mortar. This last option is perhaps easiest as you don't need to worry about a tight fit, and if one slab becomes damaged or loose it's easily removed (once the joints are raked-out) and replaced. If your paving material is precisely cut – which some modern, minimal designs can be – then it's less of a challenge to lay the elements tightly together without mortar joints.

Using mortar

Mortar differs form concrete in that it's made of sand and cement, with a little water, but contains no larger aggregate, such as gravel. The ratio of sand to cement depends on the job in hand, but for laying paving slabs a strong mix is required, so use four parts sand to one part cement.

Other methods of construction

The 'dot-and-dab' technique involves using five separate blobs of mortar (one under each corner of the slab and one in the centre) rather than a continuous bed. This saves on materials, and it's perhaps slightly easier to level the slabs, as the mortar can move more readily underneath. The problem is that very heavy rain can infiltrate through the paving joints and over time wash out or create channels in the materials underneath, which then destabilises the slabs.

Laying a stone or slab path or patio on a rigid foundation

1 With your rigid foundation in place, dry-lay the paving slabs on top to make sure you're happy with the dimensions and pattern. If you're using mortar joints, don't forget to leave even gaps in between. If any slabs need to be cut to size, do this now rather than interrupting the laying.

2 Mix up your mortar (see p58) in small batches at first, until you know how much you need for each slab. Mixing too much at once will either make you rush the job or the mortar will start to set hard before you can use it. You can mix it in an old wheelbarrow or on an old plywood board.

3 Starting in one corner of the area to be paved, spread the mortar evenly to the correct thickness. Wet the back of the first slab with a brush (this improves the adhesion of the mortar) and lay it in place. Use a spirit level and tap the slab down (allowing for the correct fall) using a rubber mallet.

4 Continue laying the first row in the direction of the slope, using spacers in between if you intend to include mortar joints. Next lay the two adjacent edges, and finally fill in towards the middle of the paving. Keep checking that the fall is correct and that each slab is flush with its neighbours.

5 If any slab rocks on its mortar bed, take it up and relay it immediately with extra mortar. When all the slabs are in place, leave them for 48 hours before you walk on them. If the weather looks likely to be bad, cover the paving with plastic sheeting well weighted down.

6 If you left gaps for mortar joints, now is the time to point them. Brush a dry mix of three parts sand to one part cement into all the gaps and force the mix down with the edge of your trowel. Repeat three or four times, then brush away any excess and water the whole surface gently.

Laying a brick or block path or patio on a flexible foundation

1 With your flexible foundation in place and compacted to the correct level (see page 56), bed a pair of timber levelling strips into the sand so that their tops are flush with the surface. Gently scrape a long timber straight edge over the strips to make sure the surface of the sand is perfectly flat.

2 Remove the levelling strips and backfill the depressions carefully with a trowel. Do not walk on the sand, but start laying your blocks or bricks from one corner in the chosen pattern. Butt the blocks tightly together, and kneel on a wide plank to spread your weight over them as you go.

3 Lay an area of around 2m² or 3m², then compact the blocks with a plate compactor. If they end up too high or too low remove them and adjust the sand level underneath. Continue across the site, laying larger areas at a time as you get more confident of the level.

4 When the patio is complete, brush fine or silver sand across the whole surface with a broom, working it into the joints. Plate compact the whole area thoroughly one more time to settle the sand into the joints, then sweep off any excess and the job is complete.

Laying patterns for bricks and blocks

As with paving slabs there are a number of different ways in which you can lay brick or block paving. Try and find examples of different laying patterns and decide which you like the look of. Some of the more popular choices include:

■ Stretcher bond

Bricks or rectangular blocks are laid end to end in straight rows, with each row staggered so as to avoid the joints lining up. A simple, easy to lay pattern.

■ Herringbone

Successive bricks are laid perpendicular to one another to create a zigzag effect. This is particularly suited to driveways, as the paving absorbs the weight of a car more evenly. You can either work on the same axis as the borders of the paving, or else rotate the bricks 45° (although this will require more cutting or bricks).

■ Basketweave

A very attractive and ornamental choice in which the bricks are laid in parallel pairs with each pair rotated 90° compared to the pair before. One of the easiest patterns to lay.

Rainwater and drainage

During heavy rainfall, the run-off of rainwater from hard surfaces such as roofs, driveways and paved areas can quickly overwhelm the ability of the surrounding soil to soak it all up. This is becoming a serious issue in urban areas, where drains, sewers and eventually our natural watercourses are forced suddenly to deal with the full volume of a downpour, rather than a gradual flow of water percolating through the soil. In other words, while the natural order of things is for rain to fall on soil then slowly be released to streams and rivers, we have created a situation in which a huge amount of water is rapidly poured into those same streams and rivers in a very short space of time. This has been the cause of many recent floods, and the law has been changed to prevent people from draining their hard landscaping – driveways in particular – on to public highways and thus into public sewers.

The good news is that paving manufacturers have been quick to come up with solutions, such as permeable materials that allow rainwater to pass straight through them and into the soil beneath, or cleverly-designed plastic foundation blocks which lock together to take the place of hardcore and concrete foundations. This last innovation can carry precipitation to a soakaway, or even to a large underground water storage tank from which it can be pumped for use around the garden.

Decking

Timber surfaces can make a beautiful and long-lasting contribution to many gardens, and can be used in much the same way as paving to extend your living space. Building a deck is also a comparatively low-cost way of landscaping an area and will take years of abuse with relatively little basic maintenance. This is not to say that you should skimp on the budget – cheap materials can lead to a cheap-looking end result, so go for the best timber and fixings you can afford.

Although wood is a natural material, the uniform look of decking is far from organic. This allows you to play with the contrast between the clean lines of the deck and the more random form of surrounding planting. Allow the two to mingle by using creeping plants and overhanging branches.

The construction of decking presents you with several choices. One idea is to build a frame of beams and suspend the joists between them, so that the top edges of beams and joists line up. This has the advantage of offering a shallow profile that allows the surface to remain close to the surrounding ground level. Another method is to lay the joists across (ie on top of) a frame of beams – stronger and easier to build, but up to twice as deep.

You also have a choice between flattening the ground and laying your timber beams on top, or installing regularly-spaced timber posts (set in concrete-filled holes) and fixing your beams to these so that whole structure is raised off the ground. This last option is the easiest if the ground is strongly sloping or uneven, but it does raise the deck above the surrounding garden and you may require steps to get back down to ground level.

Balustrading

One finishing touch well worth considering is a timber balustrade to define the edge of your deck. If you want to add one of these it's best to install the structural parts (ie the main upright posts) after the frame of the deck has been built but before you add the decking boards. Once the structure is in place you can lay the decking boards, then go back and add a top and bottom rail and the balusters themselves. Many large DIY stores and some garden centres provide all the elements required, including a range of specialist fixings. On raised timber decks, or those that border any significant water feature, a balustrade is also an important safety feature.

Building a simple deck

1 Use timber stakes and taut string lines to mark out the area to be covered by the decking. Remove any turf and other plants, plus 50mm of topsoil, then lay a water-permeable, weed-suppressing membrane over the whole site. Cover this with 50mm of gravel raked out evenly.

2 On top of the gravel lay out four treated timber deck joists to make the outer edges of the deck. Make sure the corners are square, then use two coach screws to hold each join together. Pre-drill the holes, and for a neat finish use a counter-sink drill bit so that the coach screws are hidden.

3 Inside this frame, space more parallel deck joists with 400mm between the centres of each neighbouring pair. Use two coach screws to fix each end of each joist in place as you did at the outer corners. If you want to add a balustrade (see below) now's the time to do so.

4 Finally, lay your decking boards in place, perpendicular to the joists beneath. Fix each one in place using two deck screws at each joist. Leave a gap of 3mm between each board and the next – a 3mm screw is a handy spacer. Paint any cut ends with an end-grain preservative.

Walls

One of the most permanent features in a garden, brick or stone walls take some effort to install but will require only occasional maintenance and will last a lifetime. Even the simplest construction requires some skill, so if you're new to bricklaying you may be well advised to ask someone with more experience to do the work. By acting as their helper you'll be able to pick up the techniques involved.

A low, freestanding wall can be used to create an elegant boundary between different areas of the garden, perhaps a patio and lawn. A more robust construction is a good method of holding back soil and creating terraces on a sloping site. Walls around the outside of the garden can give great privacy and a sense of seclusion, but obviously the higher you build, the stronger the wall must be.

The same planning rules apply for walls as for other built structures, so be sure to check these with your local authority before starting work. The last thing you want is to have to take down all those carefully laid bricks. See Chapter 1 for more on planning.

Building with bricks

Modern bricks are uniform in size and quality, which makes bricklaying a much easier job than it once was. Unless designed for some special purpose, bricks measure 215mm long by 102.5mm wide by 65mm deep. Add to these dimensions a standard 10mm width of mortar and you arrive at 225 by 112.5 by 75mm, which is a very convenient ratio of 3:2:1. In other words laid bricks, including their mortar, are precisely twice as long as they are wide and three times as long as they are deep. This is no accident and greatly reduces the number of cut bricks you'll require while bricklaying.

Older bricks, made to Imperial measurements and varying greatly in quality and size, can still be bought from reclamation yards and reused. Those made by a single manufacturer will tend to be modular in the same way as modern designs, but each manufacturer had a different idea of what the 'correct' dimensions should be.

Hence a hard and fast guide to dimensions is impossible. Their disparate nature also makes such bricks harder to work with, and they'll resist the weather less well, but they can be very beautiful if laid by a proper craftsman. Recycling old bricks is also a green option, as you're cutting down on waste and avoiding the need for new production.

There are different types of brick, each suited to a specific purpose. 'Common bricks', in some places called 'flettons', tend to be the most cost effective but are unlikely to provide the most attractive finish. They're fine for constructions that need to be more practical than ornamental, or where they'll be concealed by some form of render or cladding. 'Face bricks', as the name suggests, are used to create a more presentable finish and will usually be rather more expensive than 'commons'. Lastly there are 'engineering bricks', which are much denser and therefore stronger than the other kinds. They're expensive, but will last much longer in difficult conditions.

For garden landscaping purposes common bricks are suited to storage sheds and other structures not generally intended for display, face bricks are a more expensive choice for high-budget structures and imposing boundary walls, while the engineering variety is best for paths and patios (as they resist frost and absorb less water, so inhibiting moss and algae growth), and for strong retaining walls and foundations.

In addition to the standard rectangular shape, there are other bricks designed for special purposes. 'Bull-nosed' bricks are curved at one or both ends, while 'plinths' are angled at the top of one end to allow the wider base of a wall to step neatly inwards to a narrower construction above. 'Bats' are likely to be the most useful, though – they're half as long as the normal brick and allow the bricklayer to fill the inevitable gaps at the end or corner of a wall. If you prefer to avoid the expense of buying bats you can make your own by cutting standard bricks in half using a lump hammer and brick bolster. A helpful supplier might even give you a pile of broken bricks to use for this purpose.

Foundations for bricklaying

As with paths and patios, a brick wall or other construction depends on the strength of its foundations for its durability and solidity. The necessary depth and width of your foundation will vary with the type of subsoil and the weight of the construction above. Remember that 'made up' or otherwise unstable soil will require you to build larger foundations than those described here.

For a typical garden wall made from a single width (or 'skin') of bricks and up to 1m tall, a concrete strip with a minimum depth of 150mm and a width of 300mm will be fine. For a wall two bricks thick you should increase these dimensions to 300mm and 450mm respectively. Taller walls, between 1m and 2m in height, will require still larger foundations, up to 450mm deep and 600mm wide. This is no place for guesswork, so even if you intend to do the work yourself you should ask for expert advice on the size of foundation required.

Marking and excavating

It's very important to get the foundations for brickwork accurately positioned, and this means marking them out and digging very carefully. When you've decided where your wall will run, check that there are no underground obstacles such as pipes or power cables. Your house deeds may be helpful here, as may a word with your neighbours about where they believe such services lie.

Digging the trench

Use a sharp spade to slice neatly down the ends and sides of your trench. The soil will mostly need to be disposed of, but keep a little for backfilling around the wall when it's built. The depth of your trench will depend on the scale of your footings, and you should allow an extra depth of two bricks so that the footings are hidden below ground. As you work you should regularly measure the sides of the trench with a spirit level to ensure that they're vertical, and as you reach the required depth you should also use a spirit level to ensure that the bottom is horizontal.

Creating the foundation

Foundations for walls are usually made from a single layer of concrete, but if you want extra strength (for example if you're worried about the stability of the ground) then you could dig a little deeper and add a layer of crushed, compacted hardcore. The composition of the concrete used in the foundation can be either; one part cement, 2.5 parts sharp sand and 3.5 parts 20mm gravel, or one part cement and five parts all-in ballast.

Mix the concrete and pour each batch into the trench, being careful not to damage the side walls. Spread and compact as you go to ensure there are no major air gaps. Do this all in one go, rather than pouring a few loads one day then coming back a few days later to finish off. This ensures that the concrete bonds together as a single layer.

A spirit level on a straight piece of timber will help you level the top surface of the foundation. Alternatively you could use marker pegs driven in every metre or so (before the concrete is poured, of course). There's no need to include a fall as there's little horizontal surface area to collect rain and drainage is therefore not so important. Allow the concrete in your foundation at least 48 hours to set hard before building on top.

Setting out a wall

1 Timber profiles are used to mark out your wall. Make your own profiles using three lengths of 25mm by 50mm timber for each. Two of these should have one end sharpened so they can be driven vertically into the ground, then the third is nailed to them and acts as a crosspiece.

2 Using a lump hammer, drive a profile into the ground approximately 400–500mm from each end of the intended wall – so you'll need a pair of profiles for each straight section of wall. Make sure both crosspieces are horizontal, and that they are exactly level with each other.

3 Working gently so as not to adjust the position of the profiles, and measuring from the centre line of your intended wall, hammer two nails into the top of each crosspiece to represent the foundation width. Tie taut string lines around the corresponding nails and peg to the ground.

4 Use a spirit level to measure vertically below your string lines, and transfer their positions on to the ground below. You can mark these lower lines using more string, marker spray paint or a line of stakes. Remove the upper lines and you're ready to start digging.

Laying bricks

Unless you have previous experience of brickwork, you may want to consider asking a professional for help. It's a difficult skill to master and it's very easy for the efforts of a beginner to look terrible. That said, if you can work slowly and carefully and are prepared to take down a few hours' work and start again if you get it wrong, then the best way to learn is often to have a go.

As the first two courses of our wall will be at least partly below ground level, build them with stronger engineering bricks so that they can resist the damp and frost. The courses above can be made from face or common bricks according to the purpose and location of the wall. Some bricks have a hollow in their top surface, which is often referred to as a 'frog'.

Bricklaying bonds

The pattern in which you lay bricks is known as a 'bond'. There are several different bonds, some easier to lay, some stronger, some suited to double-skin walls, and so on. The long side of a brick is called the 'stretcher', and the shorter end is called the 'header'. There are three main bonds used in garden construction, as follows:

STRETCHER BOND

All the bricks are laid end to end, with their long faces exposed. The courses are staggered by half a brick so that the joints between bricks are not directly above those of the course below. Bats (half bricks) are laid to fill the gaps that occur in every second course at the end of the wall, and if the wall turns a corner then stretchers and headers alternate. This bond is used only for single-skin walls (unless you want to join two skins together using wall-ties) and is not a particularly pretty finish. It's quick to lay, however, and you'll only need around 60 bricks per square metre of wall.

ENGLISH BOND

Suitable only for a double-skin wall, this attractive and sturdy method uses alternating courses of stretchers and headers. In order to avoid mortar joints lining up, the headers are displaced by one half of their width, allowing them to sit centrally above the joints in the course below. To fill the resulting gaps at each end or corner, 'queen closers' (bricks cut in half along their length) are inserted after the first header. This bond requires around 120 bricks per square metre.

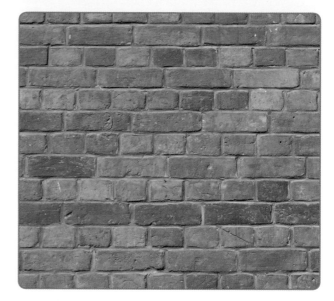

FLEMISH BOND

Yet more decorative, each course is made up of alternating headers and pairs of stretchers. The courses are staggered and, as with English bond, queen closers are used to align the bricks so that each one sits squarely above the joints below. This is the strongest of the three common bonds and requires roughly 120 bricks per square metre.

Pointing

After laying the bricks but before the mortar has set too hard, you must point the joints between the bricks. This simply means tidying and smoothing the mortar so that it excludes the weather and looks attractive. Push your thumb into one of the joints; if it leaves an impression but the mortar doesn't stick to it, then you should start pointing.

All you do is scrape along each joint so that the mortar is evenly spread, with no gaps or excess spilling out. Aim to leave a slight concave recess in the mortar so that the faces of the bricks stand slightly proud. The rounded corner of a trowel is OK for this job, but you can buy a special pointing tool. Likewise you can use a piece of dowel, an old bucket handle, or whatever you feel comfortable with.

Once the joints have hardened a little more, brush over the surface of the wall to remove any loose 'crumbs' of mortar, being careful not to dislodge the joints themselves.

Finishing a wall

To make the top layer of your wall more attractive, not to mention weatherproof, you should top it with slabs, shaped bricks or standard bricks laid on edge. Stone or concrete slabs can provide extra seating on top of a low wall, and are the easiest to use. Simply lay them end to end on a bed of mortar and ensure they're flat and level. Those that overhang are called 'coping', while those that are flush with the wall are called 'capping'.

Shaped bricks or 'coping stones' are available in a range of sizes and styles. They typically have a ridge along their centre to shed rainfall to either side. Lay and point them just as you would normal bricks.

If you've built a double-skin wall, you can top it with a final course of bricks laid across the wall, on their sides so as to hide their frogs. Use very strong mortar whatever method you choose, as the top course of a wall is often exposed to the most wear and tear.

Laying a simple brick wall

1 Using the same profiles with which you marked the foundations, tie string lines to the inner two nails and transfer to the ground below using a spirit level. A soft pencil can be used to mark the top surface of the concrete foundation. Join up your marks with a long ruler or straight edge.

2 Scoop up a trowel of mortar and drop it into place at the end of the wall, between your pencil lines. Use repeated stabbing motions with the point of your trowel, moving backwards to form a furrow in the centre of the mortar and a ridge at either side.

3 Lay the first brick firmly on the mortar so that its edge lines up exactly with your pencil mark. Use a small spirit level to ensure it's horizontal in both directions, and tap down the corners with the handle of your trowel to correct any slope. Clean off any excess mortar below.

4 Use the same method to lay temporary bricks every metre along the length of the wall, using a long spirit level to ensure the tops of all the bricks are level with one another. At the far end of the wall lay the last brick, and then remove and clean the temporary bricks in between.

5 Push two line pins into the ground at each end of the wall and attach string to them to mark out the top level of the first course of bricks. Lay the remaining bricks in the first course to this line, ensuring that you work exactly to the pencil marks all the way to the previously-laid final brick.

6 Each brick needs a trowel of mortar laid on the foundation below, though you can place several trowels at a time to speed things up. Pick up each brick in turn and wipe half a trowel of mortar on the trailing end before bedding it in place. Check your joints are all 10mm as you go.

8 Repeat step 7 at the other end of the wall. Now that you've raised the ends by a few bricks you can insert your line pins in the mortar joints of the end bricks, allowing you to stretch the string lines between them to give a guide to the level of each course.

9 Check the level regularly against the lines, and make sure that the entire length of the wall is vertical using a spirit level. You'll need to point the bricks every course or two until you get faster at laying, as you need to do this before the mortar dries out.

7 Use a half brick to start the second course, then lay three stretchers centred over each joint below. Go back to the start of the wall and lay three more stretchers to start the third course, then a half brick and two stretchers to start the fourth and so on to create a series of steps.

Steps

To create a safe means of moving up or down hill in a sloping garden you may need to install steps. As with paving and decking, there are a number of design options, and you're sure to find something that will suit your overall scheme. One thing that all steps should have in common, however, is a regard for safety. Long or steep flights should always have handrails, and you should break up long runs of steps with landings (although this will only be necessary in gardens that slope very seriously). The dimensions of every step should be the same so that you walk up and down them with an even gait.

The tread of outdoor steps (that is to say the horizontal surface on which you place your feet) should be at least 300mm from front to back for comfort, and 450mm is more sensible. The risers, or vertical measurements, should be 100 to 150mm and never more than 200mm. If you have a long shallow slope it's much safer to have two level sections separated by three or four steps than to have a solitary step every couple of metres.

How many steps?

Measure the change in height that you need to overcome, using a long spirit level projecting horizontally from the top of the slope and a tape measure held vertically below this at the bottom of the slope. Divide this height by however many steps you think you'll need until you find a number that falls within the safe range for risers. Next multiply your chosen size of tread by the same number and you have the total horizontal distance.

Construction

To build masonry steps up a slope, start at the bottom. Dig out a foundation and lay the first tread flush with the ground. Steps up from paved areas can dispense with this, but those leading up from grass will otherwise quickly end up with a bare patch of earth at the bottom.

Lay courses of bricks, blocks or stone at the back edge of this base step to create the first riser, then excavate behind this and lay the foundation for the next tread. Continue upwards in the same way until you reach the top of the slope. A neat effect can be achieved by setting each tread so that it slightly overlaps the riser below, creating a lip which casts a shadow beneath – thus improving visibility.

Timber steps, for example up to a raised deck, can easily be bought as a kit. Two shaped supports sit parallel to one another, with the lower end on the ground and the upper end attached to the frame of the deck. Treads are then screwed down on to these supports from bottom to top – a very simple operation. You can also use timber to create steps set into the ground, particularly if you use very solid lengths such as railway sleepers. The construction method is much the same as with masonry steps, but you shouldn't need a foundation as the timber is flexible enough not to split or crack under pressure. This kind of material looks great in a rustic or woodland garden, with one sleeper forming each riser and packed earth or wood chip behind forming the treads. Be aware, though, that timber can become slippery when conditions are wet – you should either use very rough pieces of timber with enough natural grain to provide some grip, or else tack galvanised wire mesh over each tread.

Maintaining your hard landscaping

While they're often the most robust features in your garden, areas of hard landscaping do need occasional maintenance in order to remain in the best condition. Try and make an annual habit of inspecting timber and masonry wherever you've used it, so that you notice any problems early on. If you respond to these problems quickly they'll be much easier to deal with.

Paving

The pavers themselves are unlikely to need much attention, but if they become dirty or covered in algae you can quickly bring them round with a stiff broom and some gentle detergent. For larger jobs you may want to buy or hire a pressure washer, but you should still sweep the paving first to remove dust and grit that would otherwise leave scratches.

If any of your slabs come loose and start to rock, or become cracked or damaged, you can lift them by carefully chiselling out the surrounding mortar and prying the slab upwards with the blade of a spade. Hammer out some of the mortar left in the gap, then lay a new slab, with fresh mortar beneath, to fill the hole.

One common problem with paving is that seeds germinate in the mortar joints and weeds then grow. You must be conscientious here and pull the weeds up quickly, or their roots will soon begin to delve into the foundations and open up larger cracks. A special patio knife can be useful here, but try not to damage the remaining mortar any more than is necessary.

Decking

As it's made from timber, decking can start to dry out and crack in the sun and wind, or may start to rot if it's in a damp location. The way to deal with these problems is to rub the surface down with sandpaper and apply a new coat of preservative. This will need doing about every three years, depending on the conditions. The same is true of timber steps, balustrading and garden furniture.

Walls

Any loose or damaged coping stones or bricks can be replaced in the same way as loose paving, described above. This isn't a common problem, however. What's more likely is that the pointing between the bricks will gradually erode and crumble away. To repair this (and it shouldn't need doing more than once every ten or fifteen years), simply rake out all the loose mortar and replace with fresh.

SOFT LANDSCAPING

Soft Landscaping

Once the more permanent features of the garden are in place as discussed in Chapter 3, we can turn our attention to the more organic elements. To many people this is what 'proper' gardening is all about – the soil, grass and, of course, the plants themselves. While it's just as important to get these working well together, they're much more forgiving than any of your other design resources. Turf is fairly simple to move, remove or adjust, and plants (with the exception of large trees) can generally be moved from one spot to another. This gives you the freedom to experiment with all kinds of ideas, so don't be afraid to let your creativity loose. Garden centres, shows such as Chelsea and Hampton Court, TV gardening programmes, books and magazines, are all excellent sources of inspiration, and looking for ideas is one of the most enjoyable parts of the design process.

Lawns and turf

A central part of the majority of domestic gardens, the lawn is a multi-purpose area where people can play, entertain, eat, work and even dry the washing. It therefore sees quite a lot of traffic, and in order to remain in a healthy condition it needs a little more care than just the weekly mow.

A good lawn is achieved when the grass is growing vigorously due to healthy roots. Then, as the top growth is mown, the roots can fuel further growth. In order to reach this state, the soil should have fairly constant levels of moisture and a well-balanced supply of nutrients. While daisies and buttercups make a pretty sight, competition from such plants is bad for the grass, so decide if you want a lush green sward or a more natural, wild look. Grass roots also like a well-aerated soil, rather than compacted ground.

A summer of drought and intense use can put heavy demands on the grass, but so can a summer of excessive rain or flooding, as waterlogged soil contains little of the air that's so vital for root growth. Both conditions result in a weaker lawn, more prone to a weed or moss invasion and to pests or diseases.

To get that manicured look the secret is to mow the lawn regularly. Waiting until the grass is overgrown and scruffy will not only make extra work, it can actually harm the turf. Get into a routine and reap the rewards.

A lawn-care routine

■ MOWING

Start mowing your lawn as it begins to grow in March or April, but set the mower blades to their highest setting to avoid damaging the new root growth. Continue to mow the grass every week if conditions allow, but as the grass grows more vigorously in May and June you can gradually lower the mower blades. A normal general-purpose lawn can be cut to about 2.5cm but a finer ornamental lawn can be cut at 1.5cm in peak growing conditions. The cut grass should be collected and removed each time in order to avoid a build-up of dead grass, known as thatch.

■ WATERING

Modern grass seed mixtures are often designed to cope with some degree of drought, but a long, hot summer can still leave your lawn looking sorry for itself. Water as little as you think you can get away with, and do so last thing in the evening to reduce wastage through evaporation. A sprinkler, carefully positioned to cover only the grass, is an excellent way to ensure an even supply.

■ FEEDING

You can nourish grass regularly through the growing season with a special summer feed that supplies nitrogen to promote lush, green growth. As growth slows down later in the year, less nitrogen is required. An autumn feed provides a balance of low nitrogen with phosphorus and higher potassium to promote winter hardiness. Apply as a liquid feed or as granules, by hand or using a spreader at the rate recommended by the manufacturer, and water the lawn afterwards.

■ SCARIFYING

Most lawns acquire a layer of thatch (composed of dead grass and other debris) by the end of summer, and this will prevent air or water penetrating the soil below and so weaken the grass. A spring-tined rake used vigorously in the autumn will remove this. You can also hire a powered lawn scarifier to do a more thorough job; don't be worried if your lawn looks a mess afterwards, as it will soon recover.

Laying turf

1 Dig over the entire site to break up the soil and remove any stones, weeds and roots. Rake the surface flat. For a really smart finish, use marker pegs (as described in Chapter 3) to ensure the ground is completely level.

2 Walk along one edge of the lawn with your weight on your heels to compress the soil and squeeze out any air gaps. Repeat across the lawn to prevent uneven settlement. Rake over again to lightly break up the surface.

3 This is a good time to apply a slow-release fertiliser to give the grass a good start. This is often sold as pre-seed fertiliser and should be spread evenly over the soil according to the instructions on the packaging.

4 Where possible, start by laying a line of turf all around the perimeter of your lawn. This avoids any edge ending up with a thin strip of turf along it, which could quickly dry out or start to break down and migrate.

5 Next work back and forth across the plot, laying the strips of turf tightly together. When you reach the end of the row, cut neatly and start the next row with the offcut. This prevents the joins from lining up and minimises waste.

6 When the turf is all in place, use the back of a rake to tamp down the edges neatly and to make sure there's good contact with the soil beneath. Work from a wooden board rather than standing on the fresh turf.

■ AERATING

Frequent foot traffic and regular mowing will slowly compact the soil under your lawn, and this is bad for the grass. In areas of particularly heavy use this can cause the roots to die and bare patches to appear. To combat this process you should aerate the soil at least one a year; autumn is a good time, as the soil is damp enough to work but not so wet as to be too heavy.

The simplest method of introducing air into the soil is by plunging a garden fork deep into the soil at 10–15cm intervals, giving it a wiggle and then pulling it out again. Hollow-tine aerators are also available – these remove a soil plug, so creating a bigger air channel. Again, both methods are suitable for small areas, but the process is particularly laborious on large lawns or in sticky clay soils, so consider hiring a mechanical aerator.

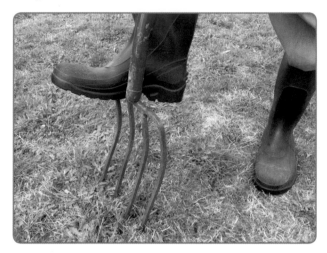

■ TOP DRESSING

Once your lawn is aerated you can improve its long-term health by brushing a mixture of six parts sand, three parts garden soil and one part compost over the turf and into the newly-opened air channels. This will help both aeration and drainage. Use about 3kg per square metre.

Dealing with lawn pests

Grass is pretty robust stuff, but there are a couple of pests to watch out for. Often the only signs of attack are poor growth and yellow-brown patches in the lawn during summer. If you're sure the family dog is not to blame, the damage could be caused by root-eating leather jackets or chafer grubs. These pests are the larval form of crane flies (leather jackets) and the cock chafer beetle (chafer grubs). Both larvae eat the roots of grass, then pupate and emerge as adults. They return to the lawn to lay their eggs and the cycle continues. Both these pests can be dealt with by applying a parasitic nematode (a tiny creature that kills the larvae).

The other turf-based troublemaker is the mole. Notoriously difficult to deter, moles are in fact a sign of a healthy lawn. The soil in a molehill also makes great potting compost, so maybe they just have to be tolerated!

Growing a lawn from seed

1 Dig over the entire site to break up the soil and remove any stones, weeds and roots. Rake the surface flat. For a really smart finish, use marker pegs (as described in Chapter 3) to ensure the ground is completely level. Walk along one edge of the lawn with your weight on your heels to compress the soil and squeeze out any air gaps. Repeat across the lawn to prevent uneven settlement. Rake over again to lightly break up the surface. This is a good time to apply a slow-release fertiliser to give the grass a good start. This is often sold as pre-seed fertiliser and should be spread evenly over the soil according to the instructions on the packaging.

2 If sowing by hand, mark out 1m² metre on the soil using bamboo canes or pegs and string. Measure out the correct amount of your chosen seed and spread evenly in the square. This will show you how densely to sow across the rest of the lawn.

3 If using an automatic seed spreader (these can be hired), set it to release the correct amount of seed, fill the hopper and walk it back and forth across the soil. Drop spreaders are more accurate than spinning ones.

4 Working from one side of the plot to the other, lightly rake the seed into the surface. This also helps remove footprints and wheel marks. In dry conditions you should now water the seed in, and keep it moist until established.

Creating a new lawn

Sometimes an existing lawn has been neglected and is in such bad condition that the best option is to dig it up and start again. On other occasions a new lawn may be required where previously none existed, perhaps where a flower bed or shed has been removed to create more open space. Either way your options are to sow grass seed over the area and wait for it to grow, or to lay strips of turf to create an instant effect.

As well as giving quicker results, turf is also less prone to bird damage and the effects of drought, and is perhaps easier to use and more likely to give good results. It can be laid all year round (although spring and autumn are the best times), whereas grass seed is prone to failing if sown in summer and not well watered. Turf, however, is much more expensive to buy, so if you have the time and are on a budget seed is the way forward.

Grass seed and turf both come in a variety of mixes, and you should buy one that suits the use you intend for your lawn. Hard-wearing, fine, general-purpose and shady lawn mixes are commonly available, with each containing a slightly different mix of grass species.

Take it easy

There are a number of specialist lawn-care companies who will take the strain out of caring for your lawn. They will charge a monthly or annual fee and will professionally perform all of the maintenance tasks described above, plus diagnose and treat any pest problems for you. Costs will vary with treatments and lawn area, but prices can start at as little as £2 per week or £13 per treatment for an average lawn of 100m^2.

Restoring bare patches

Most bare patches will probably be caused by compaction, so make sure that this is addressed before repairing the lawn. The area can be either sown with grass seed or patched with turf, but try to match the grass mix to the original in the lawn.

To reseed, gently fork over the soil and rake it level, then firm down gently. Water the area, then sprinkle on the seed to give an even coverage of up to 20g per square metre and gently rake the area again. Cover with fleece, clear plastic or taut strings to reduce losses to birds.

To repair a worn patch with turf, cut out an area around the bare patch using a half-moon cutter against a timber board. Lift the turf by undercutting with a spade. Fork over the soil, rake level, and lightly firm before placing down a new piece of turf. Trim the turf to fit snugly against the cut edges then water well and regularly.

Beds and borders

If acres of stone and timber don't fit with your idea of a paradise garden, don't despair. Once the permanent structures are in place you can begin to add plants. Start with the larger specimens, such as any trees that will form the basic skeleton of the display. In a formal plot you'll want to place these symmetrically, but in an informal, cottage-style garden you might prefer a more random approach. Either way, the same basic planting rules apply. The taller trees will need to be at the back of the borders, with shrubs and taller perennials in the middle, gradually sloping down to low-growing and ground-cover plants at the front.

Do your research before you head off to the garden centre, to find out what the height and spread of the plants you're considering will be over the next few years. This is vital in order to help you to avoid costly errors. If your garden lacks privacy then fast-growing plants may seem appealing in the short-term, but if space is limited do you really want to have to prune that rashly-bought *Leylandii* every few months?

Having to fell and dispose of an overgrown tree can involve a lot of time and money, and getting rid of an established specimen inevitably involves a lot of disruption to the surrounding area, so choosing the right options for your garden isn't a job to be rushed. Also,

note that some trees of particular value or interest are legally protected by 'tree preservation orders' (TPOs), and that all trees in conservation areas come within the domain of planning laws. So to be on the safe side, always call your local authority's tree officer and check the situation.

Be aware that large-growing trees can be very hungry feeders. Over time they can drain the soil of moisture and nutrients, meaning that you'll be very limited in your choices as to what you'll be able to grow underneath and around them. When planting close to a building or wall you also need to consider the final size of your tree. The root ball

Opening a new bed

1 Mark out the edges of your intended bed. Bamboo canes or pegs and string are OK for straight edges, while a trail of sand or a length of hosepipe are handy for curves.

2 Use a half-moon edger to cut through the turf along the marked edges. To get neat lines where the edges are straight you can cut against an old timber plank.

3 Use a sharp spade to slice under the unwanted turf. Remove one narrow strip at a time and either reuse it elsewhere or stack it out of the way to rot down.

4 Dig over the soil very thoroughly, combining garden compost or manure as you go. The more work you do to prepare the ground now, the healthier your plants will be.

(the part of the tree below ground) will be of similar proportions to the upper part, and could interfere with foundations, particularly if the tree is a thirsty one. Do your research into suitable varieties and, if in any doubt, plant at least 3m away from any such structure.

The shape in which trees grow is another factor to consider. Standard trees are 'lollipop'-shaped and will typically have a round head on top of a long thin trunk. You can often have a decent planting area underneath these types, as lots of light will reach the ground. Weeping trees, by contrast, will have lots of growth at the top of the trunk that branches down towards the earth, often obscuring the trunk of the tree and the ground beneath. These can be a very decorative focal point in the middle of a garden, but few plants will thrive in the shade that they cast. Columnar trees, such as cypresses, are often a good choice for smaller gardens, where their unusual shape can be an important part of the overall skyline. A smaller tree placed as a focal point away from the perimeter of your plot helps to provide vertical interest.

The next part of your framework to consider is your selection of shrubs, hedges and climbing plants. It's a good idea to sketch out a planting plan to give you an idea of what you'd like to put where. Consider if you want to frame a favourite view or, conversely, screen a less attractive area of the plot such as a compost heap or garage. Work in focal points, and once you've got an outline in mind you can add interest by choosing plants

with different forms and foliage types. If you select plants with leaves that are copper-coloured, variegated or silver these can bring months of interest to your plot.

You'll also need to consider the type of soil that you have. In most gardens it will be slightly alkaline, and you can grow a wide range of plants, but in some areas the soil is more acidic, which means that it's suited to lime-hating shrubs such as rhododendrons, azaleas, blueberries and camellias. If you're a fan of these plants but you don't have acid soil, you can simply grow them in large containers filled with ericaceous compost, which is readily available in garden centres.

If you put time and consideration into creating an attractive framework, it's difficult to go wrong when it comes to planting your flower borders.

Create a perennial border

Unlike annual plants, which grow, set flowers, seed and die all in one year, perennials live for many years and represent a good investment of both money and effort. Bold, mature perennials are the pride of an established garden and can really draw the eye. A large border devoted to perennial plants would once have seemed old-hat, but fashions have come full circle and such a feature is now all the rage.

Variety is the key to success here; an effective mix of shapes and sizes – or 'habits', to use the technical term – combined with a well chosen palette of colours will give a well-rounded effect. Don't be afraid to include large species, if you have the space, but make sure you allow for their final size in your planting plan. Larger plants should go at the back of the border, and your choices should gradually step down to low, spreading varieties at the front.

Colour is often the first thing that garden visitors notice, so give some thought to the flowering potential of the plants you choose. You may wish to have a powerful and vibrant display of hot summer colours in late July and August, but this will perhaps not be so attractive for the rest of the year. Alternatively you could shop for plants with a wide range of flowering times, giving interest from early spring right into autumn – good value, but lacking the impact of the summer border. When choosing colours think about the finished effect: a wild mix of every colour will look pretty, but a careful selection of blues and whites would look more subtle and stylish, while all reds and yellows would make even dull days seem summery. Some of the less obvious shades, such as creams, silvers and blacks, are also worth playing with to give a sense of contrast and depth.

Foliage plants will extend the value of the border at both ends of the growing season, providing structure and texture and acting as a background or frame for each flowering plant as it comes to the peak of its display. If you want to continue using the garden into the winter then evergreens are the obvious way forward.

The visual element of a border is not its only contribution to your design. Plants that appeal to more than one of your senses should always be top of the shopping list. If your border is adjacent to a path or patio, or even a window or door to the house, then make sure you include plenty of scented plants to fill the summer air with delight. Likewise, plants with textured or furry leaves are a great pleasure when grown within reach of passing hands. Children in particular love to see Lamb's Ears (*Stachys byzantina*) growing where they can touch them.

Container gardening

There are many advantages to growing plants in containers. Pots of flowers can be used to brighten up patios or to conceal less attractive features such as drains and pipes. By growing plants in containers you can provide exactly the sort of soil requirements that they like, and you can also restrict the spread of rampant growers such as mint that would otherwise take over. What's more, you can easily move pots around to refresh your display – perhaps emphasising certain plants when they're at their best and then placing them somewhere less conspicuous once they are past their season of interest.

One or two containers simply dotted about on a patio can look a bit sparse, while a formal row can look too regimented. For the most pleasing displays, group containers in a set of three or five, with a variation in their heights and shapes. This will give your arrangement a more natural, balanced look.

The containers you choose will be a highly visible part of your design, so don't cut corners. Select pots that match the style of your garden, and remember that plants will perform best if given the largest containers that you have room for. Smaller pots are prone to drying out very quickly, so you'll need to water them on a daily basis during the summer months. If you don't have the time or inclination to do this, you can set up a simple irrigation system, where water from a hose pipe is automatically drip fed into various containers. This is also a good option to have in place if you're going away on holiday.

At the same time, it's also vital to ensure that your pots don't get waterlogged. Most containers come with holes ready-made, but always check that they have adequate drainage and drill more holes if necessary. Always put a layer of stones or broken crocks at the bottom of each pot before filling it with compost, so that water can run away, and consider investing in 'feet' to keep your pots raised slightly off the ground.

Container plants

There are so many flowers, shrubs, bulbs and even trees that happily grow in containers that there should never be a spot in the garden that looks stark and uninteresting. Perennial plants require less attention than the rapid-growing and abundant summer bedding varieties, and they can be used to form the backbone of the arrangement. Then annuals, which will flower for months on end if fed and watered correctly, can be used to provide extra colour and interest. Summer-flowering annuals will need to be removed and added to the compost heap in winter and replaced each spring after all danger of frost has passed.

One of the main things to consider when growing plants in containers is that they'll be completely dependent on a relatively modest amount of compost to provide all their needs, so resist the temptation to cram too many plants into each pot, or they'll be in danger of drying out or being underfed. When planting up containers, always add slow-release fertiliser to the compost, as well as a generous amount of water-retaining matter. Organic alternatives for both are available. It only takes a minute or two more per pot to mix in these additives and it can make all the difference to the display you achieve and the ability of your plants to survive during dry weather. Bear in mind that any containers placed close to a wall will require regular watering even during wet weather, as not much rain will get to them.

Planting a container

1 Choose the largest container that's appropriate for your project. The more soil (and thus nutrients and water) it can hold, the happier your plants will be and the less care they'll require through the growing season.

2 Most plants hate to have their roots sat in water for too long, so ensure your container has enough drainage holes in the base. You can make more holes by drilling, with a drill bit suited to the material of the container.

3 Line the base with 25–50mm of coarse gravel or stones, then add your growing medium. Special compost for containers is available, but home-made compost can also be used. Adding a water-retaining compound is a good idea.

4 All that's left now is to add your plants. Place larger ones at the back or centre, smaller ones around these and trailing varieties right at the edge, where they'll spread and soften the edges of the container.

Perennial plants for pots

Ivy, artemisia, caryopteris, cistus, helianthemum, sedum, sempervivum, cordyline, yucca, phlomis, heuchera, cyclamen, thyme, saxifrage, dwarf hebe, euonymus, ajuga and ophiopogon can all provide years of interest when grown in containers. Most of these are evergreens, so they'll provide value all through winter, and they have the added benefit of all being quite drought tolerant.

You can add further interest by selecting variegated options, and mixing them with a few annuals for a splash of colour. Many herbs such as rosemary, thyme and sage can be grown in pots, and it's well worth placing these close to paths, as they'll release their scent every time you brush past the leaves. If you have a patio outside your kitchen door, then a selection of herbs in pots is a must-have. You'll probably want to have a few by your barbecue area too.

Annuals plants for pots

Geraniums, petunias, fuchsias, begonias, impatiens and pansies are all tried-and-tested favourites that provide abundant colour over a long period. Trays of these bedding plants can be picked up quite reasonably at garden centres and nurseries. There are also plenty of annuals that can be grown from seed planted directly in the compost in your containers. Nasturtiums, sweet peas, cosmos, sunflowers and marigolds are all very easy to grow.

Border boosters

One application of containers that many gardeners forget is to use them as border boosters. This is basically when plants are grown in pots for the specific purpose of sinking the pot into the border when the plant is in full flower to give an otherwise uninspiring area a burst of colour. When they've finished their display you can simply lift them out and put them somewhere out of the way, perhaps in a greenhouse if they need winter protection. There's a range of plants that can be grown in the conservatory or heated greenhouse and put outside during the summer when the temperature warms. Remember that it's important to keep on top of fungal and pest attacks when they're in the warm and humid environment of a conservatory or heated greenhouse.

Trees in containers

Smaller trees such Japanese maples make fantastic container specimens, although you'll need to repot them at regular intervals as they grow. Topiaried bay trees or conifers are another popular choice and they look particularly good when placed in pairs at doorways, or at the end of a path. These will require a regular trim to keep them in shape, but they have the benefit of adding interest even in the depths of winter.

There are also lots of fruit trees that have been specially developed to grow in containers. Most of these will provide a glorious show of blossom in spring as well as plenty of tasty fruit in autumn. If space is limited in your garden, look out for 'family trees' that have been grafted to provide three different varieties of fruit all from one tree.

Climbing plants

Rightly popular with gardeners, climbers add elegance, height and colour. With so many to choose from there's a variety for every situation. This group is nothing if not adaptable, but they generally need both sufficient support and space to flourish. Many have their origins as woodland plants and this is reflected in their need to have their heads in full or dappled sunlight, while their roots remain cool and shaded in fertile soil. Provided these requirements are met you'll soon be surprised by the enthusiasm with which some climbers can grow.

The sight of a mature climber such as a wisteria is certainly worth waiting for; they're capable of layering an entire garden wall or fence with an impressive display of colour backed by verdant leaves. Some, such as climbing and rambling roses, are perfect for the cottage garden, where they'll quickly make themselves at home winding up into an old tree or over a shed. Others, perhaps some of the more showy clematis, could be the centrepiece of a more modern garden design.

Sweet peas: an old favourite

Scent is also worth considering – annual climbers such as sweet peas can be so sweetly scented that they fill the whole garden with perfume. They're versatile climbers, clinging to almost any support with their corkscrew tendrils. Often grown on a wigwam of bamboo or willow, they're also quite happy scrambling up a trellis, netting or through shrubs. If the supports are smooth (like bamboo) it may be worth wrapping them in netting so that the plants can get a grip.

Sweet peas don't like their roots disturbed and are best sown in early spring into bottomless pots (toilet roll tubes are ideal). Alternatively, sow direct and protect with cloches or fleece until frosts have passed. For an earlier display it's possible to overwinter your seedlings in a cold frame, in which case you'll need to get sowing in autumn. Whatever your method of propagation, it's worth feeding the plants every two weeks to encourage the best display.

Plants for architectural interest

■ Agave
Requiring full sun and well-drained soil, agaves often do well in containers on a hot patio.

■ Bamboo
There are many types to choose from, including some with striking black stems. Best kept in a pot as can be very invasive.

■ Canna Lily
The large, exotic leaves and spectacular flowers are a winning combination. They may need winter protection in colder areas.

■ Eucalyptus
An excellent option for the low-maintenance garden, and an easy way to give your garden a sense of chic elegance.

■ Tree Fern
Surely the ultimate for a tropical feel. Now widely available, these plants require some shade and a sheltered position.

Gardening for wildlife

For many people the pleasure of a garden is doubled by the birds and animals it can attract, and gardening for wildlife has become a cause célèbre in recent times. The creation of a thriving wildlife garden is hardly rocket science. Animals want much the same things as we humans – food, water, shelter and sex. Simply give them the resources they need to live a happy life and you're pretty much guaranteed to be rewarded with their presence.

To attract the greatest diversity of species, aim to provide a wide range of habitats and food sources. A well-planted pond is perhaps the single most important feature, providing a home to frogs, newts and countless insects, as well as water for birds and mammals. A few trees can offer woodland edge conditions for birds, while an area of lawn given over to native wildflowers is ideal for meadow-dwelling moths, butterflies and small rodents.

Wildlife gardens can certainly be beautiful, but they shouldn't be over-tidy. A nettle patch, rock pile and a stack of logs will soon be buzzing with life if left undisturbed for a month or two, and fading summer plants are best left in place through the winter

to provide food and shelter. With very little effort you'll soon find your garden transformed into a haven for nature.

As well as providing interest from your window, encouraging wildlife is beneficial to your plants and soil. Bees and butterflies aid pollination, whilst frogs and hedgehogs control pests. A balanced ecosystem is the key to a healthy garden – but don't think that you have to create a wilderness to attract animal life. A careful choice of plants and the addition of a small pool can invite hundreds of species to your doorstep.

If you grow vegetables you may be worried about insects on your crop. However, sowing flowers in your kitchen garden can encourage useful creatures such as the hoverfly. Attracted by the flowers, they will lay eggs on your produce and the hungry larvae will prey upon pesky aphids.

The popularity of organic methods has led to a renewed interest in companion planting. Rather than using pesticides that disrupt the natural balance of the ecosystem, aim to confuse potential pests with strong-smelling plants. Grow marigolds alongside your tomatoes to deter whitefly, or try nasturtiums with your cabbages to stop caterpillars from feasting on your produce. For a combination that's practical as well as beautiful, sow red-flowered nasturtiums against the deep green leaves of your cabbages.

Attracting bees

Bees are essential in the garden for pollinating both vegetables and ornamentals. The larvae are raised during the spring, and require the protein and fats provided by pollen. Try to avoid mowing the lawn and tidying too early in the year, as bees will appreciate the odd weed flower as a source of food – violets, clover and dandelions are among their favourites. A meadowland mixture provides nectar all year long. Sow in spring for summer flowers and next year you'll be rewarded with wild flowers in spring, summer and autumn. It isn't necessary to have a huge swathe – the mix can be used to fill gaps in the border, or to create a single patch. It's advisable to avoid sowing seeds in shadier areas – bees love the sunshine and may ignore plants situated in dark corners.

Butterflies and moths

There are over 50 different species of butterfly in the UK, although they're sadly becoming a rare sight. Careful planting can help encourage these beautiful creatures back into your garden. Buddleia is a superb choice, as the flowers are full of nectar. Earlier in the year, aubretia provides an abundant food source for butterflies emerging from hibernation.

Top five annuals for insects

■ **Pot marigold**
(*Calendula officinalis*)
Flowers from May right through until the first frosts.

■ **Poached egg plant**
(*Limnanthes douglasii*)
One of the best for attracting hoverflies.

■ **Cornflower**
(*Centaurea cyanus*)
Hoverflies love the flowers, birds go for the seed heads.

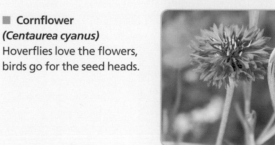

■ **Field poppy**
(*Papaver rhoeas*)
Freely self-seeding and great for bees and hoverflies.

■ **Forget-me-not**
(*Myosotis arvensis*)
A good choice for damp sites. Much-loved by bees.

Laying out a kitchen garden

One of my favourite gardening projects is designing a new vegetable patch. The best plans take into consideration the existing site and its limitations, as well as its advantages. Unlike a purely ornamental garden access is a fundamental issue, as you'll need to be able to harvest, sow, dig and plant throughout the season. Paths and walkways are important, as there's nothing more frustrating than building your perfect plot only to find that your wheelbarrow is too wide to pass the first bed!

The orientation of your plot is very important, and will help you to decide where to situate your vegetable beds and what to plant in them. A vegetable bed on a south-facing site will be very productive but can tend towards dryness during the summer. You might therefore include an automatic watering system in your design to reduce your workload. A plot that faces west will receive warm sunshine during the afternoon but may be very windy, so it will be useful to feature wind-breaking screens and plant supports in your plan. An easterly aspect could lead to a design featuring a glass-topped box for tender plants – this would retain heat from the morning sun. North-facing gardens are the hardest to manage, but you can

make them productive if you concentrate on leafy veg that will grow quickly to make use of the low light levels.

Avoid the temptation to place your vegetable plot at the bottom of the garden out of sight, unless this really does

offer the best growing conditions. Although the kitchen garden is a practical area of the garden, there's no reason why it can't also be attractive. A dark, dingy corner will mean struggling plants and poor yields. Also, low-lying parts of the plot are more susceptible to frost, as cold air can become trapped against a fence or the side your house if it has nowhere else to go. If you're a fan of ornamental plants, it can be difficult not to begrudge giving up a spot in full sun. However, when harvest time rolls round and you're picking your own fresh, organic produce you'll be glad you made the sacrifice!

The fragrant garden

Balmy summer evenings are best enjoyed with a long, cool drink in a scented garden. There are a great many plants to choose from, but there are a few old favourites that it's hard to ignore. Lavender has long been recognised as one of the most pleasant-smelling plants in the garden. A key ingredient in aromatherapy, it's said to relieve stress and promote sleep. If space is limited, the dwarf variety 'Munstead' is superb for filling gaps in the border.

As the light fades, so too will many of the flowers in your garden. If you choose your species carefully, however, your balcony, deck, or patio can retain an exotic atmosphere well into the night. Nicotiana is one of the most beautiful plants for evening scent – 'Eau de Cologne' offers a glowing palette of colours with upward facing blooms. Their uniform height range makes them ideal for inclusion in formal planting schemes. 'Fragrant Cloud' is another good variety that exudes perfume as night falls.

For a touch of classic evening glamour, try night-scented stocks. *Matthiola bicornis* bears rich pink and magenta blooms and can be sown direct in its final position. To get the best from your scented plants, situate them near the back door or kitchen window and enjoy their perfume wafting through on the breeze.

Maintaining your borders

If you're the proud owner of an established garden, you may be disappointed to see your borders looking a little tired, sprawling or straggly after a few years of growth. The answer is to divide some of your plants to rejuvenate them. What's more, it costs nothing and requires minimal equipment.

After four or five years, many varieties begin to die from the inside (the oldest part of the plant). As well as leaving unsightly gaps in the border, old and tired plants can be a magnet for pests and disease, which will then spread throughout the garden. Division is a method of propagation in which the dead and weak parts of the plant are removed and the new shoots replanted. Many familiar perennials such as hostas, aquilegia, delphinium and rudbeckia are suitable for division. In fact, most clump-forming plants can be easily divided to produce more plants.

The ideal time to get started is early spring – this allows the plants to recover while the soil is moderately warm and before the growing season begins. Large well-rooted clumps are best removed from the border with a fork or spade, and split apart. It may seem brutal, but when freed from the tangle of roots the newly-divided plants will really begin to flourish.

A large mat of tangled roots can usually be split into at least four new plants without compromising the essential root-structure. Simply transplant the divisions, discarding any obviously dead or diseased portions. Some varieties, such as hostas, develop thick gnarled roots after a few years' growth, making them impossible to split with a spade or trowel. In this case a strong, serrated kitchen knife is invaluable for slicing through the tough root ball. Less vigorous perennials need not be dug out in this way,

and it may be easier to simply remove strong, new growth with a knife before replanting each piece. The dead central portions of the plant can simply be added to the compost heap, unless they show signs of disease.

Plants with rhizomes, corms or bulbs (swollen roots), such as gladiolus, iris and crocosmia, can also be divided, although the process is slightly different. Over the course of a few seasons, these plants will begin to form additional tiny bulbs. Gladioli, for example, produce little outgrowths known as 'cormlets'. These miniature versions of the parent usually require a couple of years' growth before they'll flower, but will reach maturity more quickly if they're given easy access to nutrients, light and water. Separating and planting them a distance away from the parent means that they won't have to compete, and can therefore grow unchecked.

Plants that sprout from rhizomes, such as bearded iris, require different treatment. The long tuberous roots should be lifted as soon as the plant has finished flowering, and the young rhizomes cut off cleanly with a sharp knife. The next step is to replant so that the top of the rhizome sits very slightly above the soil.

Whichever method of division you choose, it's important to get your new plants off to a flying start. Water them in well, as the new divisions will take a while to establish a fully functioning root system. It's also a good idea to revitalise the soil with well-rotted organic matter, such as home-made compost or organic fertiliser. This is particularly important if you're planning to replant in the same spot after dividing your plants.

Hanging baskets

Hanging displays are a great way to bring a splash of colour to an otherwise uninspiring part of your garden. They can also attract flying insects, including bees, butterflies and hoverflies, to areas that might not otherwise be able to support them. Plant them up in early spring to give the plants a head start, then keep in a light, frost-free place until May. Hang a pair filled with scented flowers beside your front door and enjoy them every time you pass.

Tips for healthy baskets

■ To make life easier for your plants, use the largest size of basket you can find. It will hold more soil and water, and give room for extra root growth.

■ You may need to water twice a day in hot weather. Lighten the load by mixing a water-absorbing compound with the compost. This soaks up lots of water and then releases it slowly.

■ Use a mixture of plants, but don't get carried away with colour. A combination of just two, or several shades of the same one will have a more pleasing effect.

■ Trailing plants such as lobelia are ideal for the edges of the display – they'll cascade happily downwards and hide the container from view.

■ Use taller plants such as pelargoniums or upright fuchsias to give body to the centre of the basket.

■ Support the basket in the top of a bucket while planting – this will stop it rolling around as you work.

Using loose aggregates

Not all landscaping is firmly fixed in place. Loose aggregates, as the name suggests, are particulate materials that are simply spread in a layer on the ground. A common and traditional example would be gravel, but wood chip, shredded bark, crushed shell and even ground polished glass or chipped rubber are possibilities. The result is a pleasingly textured area that can be used for seating, entertaining, or any other purpose fulfilled by stone paving or timber decking. The construction is by no means as permanent as such hard landscaping options, but the installation is much more easy and economical.

Another advantage of some loose aggregates, in particular gravel and stone chippings, is that they're noisy to walk over. Use them close to your house to give added security – anyone crossing them will immediately make themselves known.

Laying a gravel path

1 Carefully remove any turf or weeds from the route of the path, then flatten the surface with a rake. Firm down the soil with an upended sledgehammer.

2 Loose materials need an edge to keep them in place. For prominent paths you may want to use edging stones in mortar, but a quicker option is timber boards and pegs.

3 Spread a layer of weed-excluding landscaping fabric across the base of the path. Overlap any edges by 500mm and pin in place with tent pegs or similar.

4 Cover the fabric with a layer of gravel (or other loose material of your choice) to a depth of at least 50mm. Rake flat and the path is finished.

Using mulch

Mulching is an important practice for the organic grower, yet the term can be confusing for novice gardeners. Simply put, mulching is the creation of a light-excluding layer of material around your plants. In this respect it's rather like using loose aggregates, but the materials are generally intended to rot down into the soil rather than to remain on the surface. Nonetheless, mulch can have an ornamental purpose for a limited period. It has the obvious effect of suppressing weeds, but there are many equally important benefits such as water conservation, soil enrichment and pest reduction.

Why mulch?

Since it covers the surface of the soil, a mulch will limit the amount of water lost through evaporation. When the ground is watered, the sun and wind will cause some of the water to evaporate before the plants can make use of it. A simple mulch of newspaper, shredded bark, composted leaves or organic matter such as grass clippings will therefore keep the ground moist for much longer – thus reducing your watering requirements.

Mulching can also help with soil enrichment. If you opt for a good covering of well-rotted farmyard manure or home-made compost, your plants will receive a steady supply of nutrients as worms take the organic matter into the soil. Regularly replenishing the mulch on a long-term basis will, over time, improve the structure of your soil, aerating heavy soils or improving light, sandy ones.

Which mulch?

A mulch can be composed of a variety of materials, and your choice will depend upon its intended purpose. The list below will guide you through the most common types and their uses:

- Compost – Your own home-made compost makes an effective and nutritious mulch for growing fruit and vegetables. The nutrients will be readily worked into the soil by worms, so the mulch will need to be replaced regularly. Although their appearance will be delayed, weeds will grow through easily.

- Bark – Wood chips or bark can be used as an effective water-conserving mulch. They're longer-lasting than compost, although this can be a disadvantage if a quick nutrient boost is required. Always allow wood chips to decompose on top of the soil, as they'll deplete nitrogen levels if dug in.

- Leaf mould – Leaf mould can be made by collecting and storing leaves in plastic bags. The resulting mixture is rich in nutrients and improves soil structure. However, some types of leaf (such as oak) can take up to three years to decompose before they can be used.
- Grass clippings – These make a convenient mulch since they're almost always available.
- Straw – Straw is an effective insulator, helping to retain heat during a cold spell. It is also ideal for courgettes, strawberries, raspberries, pumpkins and melons, offering a dry surface to prevent developing fruits from rotting.
- Seaweed – Whilst it may be difficult to gather sufficient quantities for weed suppression, seaweed is one of the best sources of nutrients.
- Crushed shell – Sharp, splinter-like mulches, such as broken shells or grit, can be useful for protecting crops from slugs and snails. Since these are not readily decomposed, apply a thin layer around individual plants.

Laying an area of mulch

1 Whatever your choice of mulch, it's important to clear the ground of weeds before you begin. Dig-over the soil as best you can without disturbing the existing plants.

2 Tip your chosen mulch on to the soil and spread it around and under your plants. Aim for a layer at least 5cm thick, leaving no bare soil.

3 For a neater finish you may want to rake the surface of the mulch level. This can also help you find areas where the mulch is too thin, as the soil is revealed by the rake.

4 Through the following weeks and months, keep an eye on the progress of your mulch. If you want to continue the process you can add a new layer as the first one rots away.

Trees and hedges

Two of the more substantial elements of your garden, trees and hedges are a long-term investment that will give years of visual interest. Trees can provide pleasant shade on hot summer days, which is important if you're likely to have young children playing in the garden. Delicately-leaved varieties like silver birch are good in this respect, as they don't cut out too much light. Hedges can offer security when mature, especially if you opt for dense-growing or thorny varieties.

Other advantages of both trees and hedging are that they can provide privacy from neighbours or passing pedestrians, habitats for wildlife such as birds, protection from the wind and cold weather, and even edible fruit and nuts if you choose carefully.

There are many ways to plant a hedge. The traditional methods involve complex and skilful pruning to get the plants to grow together in a dense block. This takes years of experience to get exactly right, but you won't go far wrong if you choose the right dense-growing plants and planting them close together in a line. Most shrubs and trees can be used, but if you want to combine more than one species remember that some will outgrow others; so if you want to keep things in proportion you'll have to cut the vigorous ones back accordingly.

An edible hedge

Rather than use functional but bland hedging plants such as laurel or beech, why not create a hedge of fruiting plants (sometimes known as a 'fedge') to edge your garden? Even if you don't get round to picking and cooking the nuts and berries it produces, it will be greatly appreciated by your local wildlife.

One thing to remember is that these plants need to be pollinated, just like apple and pear trees. Do a little research before you start planting to ensure you have at least two examples of anything that isn't self-fertile.

Planting a tree

1 Dig a circular hole twice the depth and diameter of the container in which the tree is growing, or around 50cm wide and deep if the tree is bare-rooted. Keep half the soil in a wheelbarrow. Gently break up the sides and base of the excavation with a hand fork, to make it easier for the roots to spread. Pour at least one full can of water into the hole.

2 In the wheelbarrow, mix enough garden compost into the reserved soil to increase its volume by about half. Add a couple of handfuls of fertiliser such as blood, fish and bone. Drop some of the soil mix into the hole and firm down with your foot. Place the tree on top – the top of the compost around the roots should be at ground level. Adjust if necessary.

3 Making sure the trunk of the tree is straight, backfill the sides of the hole with your soil mix. Firm down as you go so that no pockets of air remain, then water the tree thoroughly.

4 Drive two long timber stakes into firm ground on opposite sides of the tree, then screw a batten between them. Use a soft tree tie or an old pair of tights to hold the trunk secure.

Plants for the edible hedge

■ **Blackthorn**
So sharp in flavour as to be almost inedible raw, sloes add a delicious twist to gin or vodka and also make a tasty jelly.

■ **Elder**
The flowers are delightful as a cordial or wine, as are the berries if you can get to them before the birds.

■ **Hazel**
Cobnuts taste amazing fresh off the branch, and many hazel varieties look great too.

■ **Sea buckthorn**
The plentiful, bright orange fruits look great all winter and are packed with vitamins.

■ **Blackberries**
Needing no introduction, blackberries will scramble happily through other plants and offer fruit from late summer through autumn.

■ **Crab apples**
Very much at home in such a setting, crab apples fruit prolifically, look beautiful in late summer and even help pollinate other apples trees. 'John Downie' has to be my favourite variety.

Maintaining a hedge

The trick to keeping a hedge in good shape is to trim it regularly – every spring and autumn. This will encourage it to form a dense and uniform body of growth rather than simply becoming a line of small trees, with spindly branches thrown out in all directions. Electric or petrol-powered hedge trimmers can save you hours of work if you have extensive hedging, but hand shears will do the job too.

Aim to make the base of the hedge slightly wider than the top, so that the sides are less than vertical. This allows the leaves at the base to receive just a bit more sunlight, which helps them to grow as healthily as those at the top.

Maintaining a tree

Trees can often be left to their own devices for many years, but there will be occasions on which it's necessary to remove a branch or two. This may simply be to keep a path or seating area free of shade or obstruction, or perhaps to remove some broken or diseased wood. Taking off a branch is not difficult, but it must be done correctly to avoid harming the tree.

Removing a tree branch

1 Use a pruning saw to make a shallow cut in the underside of the branch, around 30cm from the trunk and deep enough to sever the bark around the lower half.

2 Slightly further out from the trunk, make a cut through the branch to remove it. The earlier cut should stop the bark tearing down the trunk as the branch falls.

3 At the base of the branch you'll find a 'collar' of wood. This contains regenerative cells that will help the tree heal. Cut neatly against it, supporting the branch.

4 Cut up and dispose of the branch. Don't cover the wound but leave it to heal in the fresh air. It will quickly dry out and the tree will suffer no lasting harm.

GARDEN LANDSCAPING

GARDEN STRUCTURES

5

Garden structures

An important part of most landscaping schemes, built structures can bring a great deal to your garden. Some are almost purely ornamental and are used to give a sense of structure, define a route, or add vertical interest. Others are very practical and can be used to delineate a boundary, or store garden tools and equipment. Most have an element of both – pergolas, summer houses and sheds can all bring extra uses to your outdoor space but can also, if handled carefully, add to the visual appeal.

Decorative structures

There are a number of wooden elements that can be used in a garden to bring a sense of height and to give it that all-important 'established' feel. Pergolas, arches, arbours and seats can all be bought quite reasonably or built for an even smaller outlay. Once they're planted with decorative climbers they can look breathtaking, and if you choose evergreen climbers such as *Clematis armandii* they'll provide interest in the garden all year round. Another option is to grow complementary climbers that flower at different times of the year, or have a decorative autumn leaf-colour to prolong the seasons of interest.

Pergolas and arbours are a very popular feature in Mediterranean gardens, where they're used to provide very welcome areas of shade. In many hot countries the arbour is effectively used as a dining room all summer long, as sitting under a leafy bower offers just the right amount of dappled light, and on a hot day this spot is often far more breezy and refreshing than being stuck indoors.

Although these wooden structures look quite striking as soon as they're erected, it's when they're clothed with plants that they really come into their own. They're the ideal support for a few grapevines, or blooms such as wisteria or laburnum that hang down, making the area underneath quite spectacular to walk through.

Pergolas

The term 'pergola' is usually applied to a covered walkway, made from vertical posts supporting an open 'roof' of beams. Building a pergola can be a very effective way of joining one part of the garden to another. You can also use these structures to lead to a particular spot in the garden, such as a patio, seating area or potager.

They can be built quite simply by placing a line of posts on either side of the pathway and joining them together by putting beams on top. If you grow scented plants up the supports, such as sweet peas, jasmine or roses, then walking underneath can be even more enjoyable. If your garden isn't sufficiently large to justify creating a covered route from one part to another, you could consider creating an arbour along one side as a sort of cloister, with benches positioned in niches to create a shady spot from which to look out on the rest of the garden.

If vertical interest in the form of trees and tall shrubs is short in your garden, then make your pergolas and arches work even harder for you. They'll be a wise investment, as

Using height to your advantage

While it should be obvious that vertical elements are an important part of garden design, there's slightly more of the story to be told. By mixing features of varying heights you'll create a much more absorbing whole than if you rely only on one vertical element, such as fencing. Try to stage your design so that the tallest objects – probably trees or garden buildings – are stepped down to ground level in increments, perhaps using tall shrubs, arches and pergolas, surrounded by medium and low planting, climber-covered obelisks and seating, with spreading and ground cover plants lowest of all.

you're utilising the space far more effectively, easily getting twice the interest for your money that you would gain from a bed or border.

Upright features can be as productive as they're decorative, as many fruits and vegetables are very attractive in their own right. Experiment with kiwi fruit vines with their pretty foliage, or Japanese wineberries with their decorative red stems and mouth-watering fruit. Even old favourites such as marrows and courgettes can be trained to climb up a wooden support, and you can find mixes of runner beans with red, pink and white flowers that provide a stunning show *en masse*.

A good range of structures can be found at most garden centres or by mail order, and they're generally very simple to assemble. But if you've got basic DIY skills, there are lots of benefits to making these features yourself.

Building a timber arch

1 Drive a pair of 2,400mm pressure-treated fence posts 400mm into the ground, one on either side of your path or entrance way. Repeat with a second pair 900mm away from the first.

2 Ensure all four posts are vertical, then join their tops with 100 x 25mm timber screwed round the outside. For a more ornamental effect, project and shape the ends of those that cross the path.

3 Trellis will give your plants something to climb up. You can make your own from pressure-treated timber battens, or buy ready-made panels in 900mm widths and a range of styles.

4 If you want to make your arch blend with the surrounding garden, then a couple of coats of green or brown exterior paint are ideal. Otherwise, why not experiment with bolder colours?

Ideally you'll want your pergola to be at least 2m high, as this gives you room to walk underneath, and really makes you feel like you're in a 'garden room'. For a reasonably-priced timber construction, buy pressure-treated fence posts around 2.4m long and 75mm thick from a builders' merchant. Dig holes 450mm deep in the ground at 450–900mm intervals and use bags of ready-mixed concrete to secure the posts in place. Then attach the beams that will form the roof across the top of each two uprights. You can use straight or curved pieces of wood, but it's worth remembering that the structures will mostly only be on show until the plants have grown up over them.

Next dig holes for your climbing plants, and enrich your planting holes with plenty of organic matter such as home-made compost. To give your plants a helping hand while they're getting established, use vine eyes to fix a length of galvanised wire to each post so that the climber can be tied to it with soft string as it climbs upwards. Get into a routine of watering your climbers regularly in their first year, and use this time to look out for any new growth that needs to be tied in. If you give them a good start in this way, your care routine in the future may well be as simple as just a little seasonal pruning.

Arches

A garden arch, forming a doorway through a hedge or trellis screen, is a wonderful way of creating a sense of seclusion in one part of the garden. They're also perfect for creating a sense of drama as you leave one part of the design and step into the next. A wide arch can be used as a form of shelter above a garden seat, or immediately outside a door into the house. However, aches are generally not as substantial as pergolas and are therefore more suited to one or two delicate climbers than to a mass of rambling plants.

While pre-formed metal arches are widely available, some of them more sensibly priced than others, if you're gardening on a budget it may be better to build your own out of timber. The result doesn't even have to be arch-shaped, but make sure it's tall enough to give unrestricted access. If you do opt for a metal design, make sure you choose one that's sturdy enough to resist a good few years of wind and rain. Too many such products are only designed to look good for the duration of their shelf life.

Plants for pergolas and arches

There are a great many climbing plants suited to training up and over your garden structures, but here are a few chosen for their foliage, flowers and scent.

■ **Sweet pea (*Lathyrus odoratus*)**
Available in a range of colours these flowers smell as good as they look.

■ **Jasmine (*J. nudiflorum, officinale*)**
Great for larger gardens or deep containers, the white flowers have a heady scent.

■ **Clematis (*C. alpina, armandii, montana, viticella*)**
Choose a montana variety if you want fast growth or armandii for evergreen leaves.

■ **Passion flower (*Passiflora caerulea*)**
Don't be fooled by their delicate looks, these easy-grow plants are tough as old boots!

■ **Golden hop (*Humulus lupulus 'Aureus'*)**
Perfect for a natural-looking cottage garden, these plants have lush green foliage.

■ **Rose (*many Rosa spp., including 'Rambling Rector', 'Paul's Himalayan Musk' and 'New Dawn'*).**
Choose climbers for arbours and ramblers to cover larger structures.

■ **Honeysuckle (*Lonicera spp.*)**
The sweetly-scented flowers are irresistible to bees, and you get berries in autumn too.

■ **Wisteria (*W. floribunda, sinensis*).**
This timeless classic can give two flushes of glorious blooms, one in May and another in July.

lines of these, planted a couple of metres apart, will quickly reach a useful height and can be pulled in from both side and tied gently together. As the side shoots develop they can be woven between the main uprights to provide more shelter. Extending the arch can give you a leafy green walkway, while weaving a circle of saplings into a dome creates a shady spot for a bench or an exciting den for kids to play in.

Remember that whatever plants you choose to grow over your arch will probably be encountered at very close quarters by those passing beneath. This presents an ideal opportunity to use scented and floriferous climbers such as clematis, honeysuckle and roses. Don't forget, however, that thorny plants can be more trouble than they're worth in such a location.

Living arches

While metal or timber arches are more common, it's possible to make an archway out of living plants. Willow is the best for this, as it's so fast-growing and flexible. Young willow saplings are available quite cheaply, or you can cut and propagate your own from a mature tree. Two parallel

Gazebos

Gazebos are usually attractive wooden structures with an enclosed roof but open sides. They offer a great place to sit and read, or perhaps enjoy a meal or a drink on a warm day. Often round or hexagonal in shape, gazebos are best sited in a spot where they can command the best views of the garden, and perhaps the surrounding area. As gazebos are designed to look decorative in their own right, you may want to consider placing one at the end of a path or vista where it will draw the eye and emphasise key features of your plot.

Practical structures

Garden composters

No garden should be without a compost bin – it gives you the opportunity to turn all your kitchen and garden green waste into lovely soil conditioner. Well-rotted garden compost is far superior to anything that can be bought from a garden centre and the only expense you'll have is the bin itself! However, due to their practical function some compost bins can, quite frankly, be a bit of an eyesore. There are several ways around this problem, and the solution you choose depends very much on the size of your plot and the style of garden you want to achieve.

If you have a limited budget for your bin, it's extremely easy to make your own from four pallets tied together in a square shape with some lengths of garden wire – the bottom of the bin area should be in contact with the soil, as hungry worms will do a great job of eating all sorts of garden waste.

The sides of the bin can be lined with a layer or two of corrugated cardboard – this helps to keep all your grass cuttings and other matter in place and also acts as a handy insulating layer. Simply open out old boxes and lean them against the edges of the pallets – they're much easier to fold and bend when slightly damp, so give them a quick hosing over if necessary. The cardboard will eventually rot down, adding its cellulose and nutrients to the rich, organic matter in your pallet bin. If you have room, you could have three of these home-made structures together, making it easy to spade the compost from one to another as it breaks down.

In some areas the council will either provide large plastic bins for free, or at a subsidised rate. These structures are very roomy, but again they aren't necessarily something that you'd want on show.

A simple solution is to site your bin in an out of the way corner where it can't easily be seen, such as behind some shrubs or under a tree. You could even erect a trellis and train decorative climbing plants such as jasmine, clematis or hops up the front. Be aware, however, that a potential disadvantage of this method is that compost bins work best in the sun. The organic matter breaks down into a lovely crumbly loam far more quickly when the heat of the sun helps the all the microorganisms inside the bin to do their helpful work rotting down the contents. If your bin is in a shady spot it can take up to twice as long for your garden waste to break down into a usable state. Fortunately, you can help out by giving the heap a regular turn, or by using special tools to help aerate the contents of the bin and thereby speed up the decomposition.

Another option is to make your compost bin into a feature in its own right. There are a number of different decorative designs on the market, including popular beehive-style bins that can be painted in natural colours to blend in with your plot, or in bold shades if you want to create an eye-catching effect. This may be your preferred option if you have limited space that would make hiding an unsightly object very difficult. An added benefit of these beehive-style bins is that they tend to come in separate sections, which means it can be very easy to get to your compost either to turn it, add to it or use it!

One rather more unusual option is to build a compost bin from bricks. If you happen to have access to some reasonably-priced bricks, or you have some left over from a building project, they can be used to make a surprisingly ornamental feature.

First mark out a circle on the soil where you want to build your bin – you could use a dustbin or similar object as a guide for the initial shape. Simply place the 'foundation' layer of bricks in a neat circle. Then, for the second layer, place each brick in a stretcher-bond fashion on top, but in a slightly tighter circle, so that you're gradually building up a cone shape that resembles an oast house.

Leave a wide hole at the top so that you can easily add all your garden waste, and to give you room to aerate the heap from time to time. When you can see that it's turned

to a rich loam, the easiest way to get to your compost is to take the whole thing down, brick by brick. This is, of course, quite time-consuming, but the advantage of this temporary structure is that you can experiment with different positions in the garden and see which works best for you.

A much less labour-intensive way to make a good soil conditioner is to rake up all your garden leaves in autumn and pop them into biodegradable sacks so that they can rot down into crumbly leaf mould. Some species are slower to break down than others, but it generally tends to take around a year for them to be transformed into a useful mulch, so again you may prefer to store these compost bags out of sight.

You can even make your own leaf mould cages by putting four stakes in the ground and wrapping chicken wire around them. Pile all your leaves inside this simple structure and pop a cardboard lid on top, made of a flattened box or two, weighted down with bricks, and by next year you'll have plenty of useful organic matter that you can add to your flower beds by the spadeful.

Sheds

If you're shopping for a new shed it's always worth getting one a size or two larger than you think you'll need, as they're incredibly practical structures and chances are you'll get tremendous use out of every bit of extra space. It's much easier to get to your lawnmower, strimmer and all the other garden tools you need if you have lots of room to arrange them in a practical layout. If you're lucky enough to have room for a comfy chair in the shed too, then make this a priority. It will give you a very welcome spot in which to have a peaceful cup of tea, to read through a seed catalogue, do a spot of potting on, or to plan your day's gardening.

Unless you're blessed with a huge plot, the chances are that your shed will be one of the most prominent features in your garden, so it's well worth doing what you can to make it look as attractive as possible. There are specialist paints and wood stains which can make a surprising amount of difference, or you could train climbing roses over the roof, or put pots or baskets of flowers at the front.

If you've already got a shed that's a bit too tatty for a makeover, the next best option is to hide it behind a trellis screen – perhaps alongside the compost bins in a separate utility area. You could even build a wood store alongside the shed and add a couple of water butts and some guttering so that you can harvest precious rainfall on the roof and use it on your plants. If your shed happens to occupy an attractive position in your garden, a bench placed in front will give you a place to sit and admire the fruits of all your hard work.

Most sheds are made of wood, and this material is understandably popular for gardens as it looks attractive and can blend in easily with your plants, trees and fences. By creating a good concrete or paved base for a wooden shed, and raising it off the ground, you can prolong its life for a number of years, as you'll prevent damp and rot from setting in.

If you're considering buying a new shed then it's worth

considering other materials, if the time spent on maintenance is your priority. Plastic sheds, for example, will never need painting and you won't need to re-felt the roof, although their ease of use is often reflected in a hefty price tag. Also expensive, metal sheds are incredibly secure, but they can look a bit industrial.

Most sheds have the same basic shapes, but there are two main roof designs. An apex roof has two sides that slope down from a central ridge – this echoes the design of most houses and can therefore feel very homely and inviting. Pent roof sheds might not look so appealing, as the roof simply slopes down from one side to the other. However, these designs tend to offer more headroom than an apex-style shed, and they're ideal if you want to place your shed right next to the wall of your house or garage, as rain will simply run off down to the outside.

The number of windows you choose in the shed can also have an impact on how it looks and the way you use it. If you don't have room for a separate shed and greenhouse on your plot, you can choose a potting shed, which will have a bank of windows right across the length of one wall. These designs often feature a bench next to the window, so you can make the most of this light space to grow your plants.

Summer houses are often very similar to a shed in their basic structure, but they tend to have lots more windows at the front and sides, which makes them an attractive place to enjoy a meal on a summer's evening.

Plant supports

While some plants are robust enough to look after themselves year in year out, others rely on help from the gardener to look at their best through the seasons. Some need artificial help to resist the effects of wind and rain, while others need you to provide something up which they can climb. In the borders, more slender and delicate plants like delphiniums often require staking or the provision of wire supports to hold them upright, and therefore visible in the surrounding vegetation.

You can buy tailor-made supports in a range of styles and sizes, but if you have a good stock of timber offcuts and bamboo canes then it's just as easy and far cheaper to make your own.

Climbing plants grown against a wall will also need some provision for support, as few will be tenacious enough to grip on to brickwork unaided. The traditional way to resolve this is to hammer or screw galvanised vine eyes into the

brickwork, and to stretch rust-resistant wires between these. While some plants will race up these wires on their own, others are less precocious and will need to be gently tied to the wires as they put on new growth. To ensure the brickwork behind has a chance to dry out after rainy weather, aim to leave a gap of at least 50mm between the wires and the wall.

Timber trellis can also be used against a wall to give support to climbing plants, but be aware that this is very difficult to maintain when covered in vegetation. It's therefore a less long-lived installation.

Greenhouses

Any keen gardener will place a greenhouse high on their list of important projects. For starters it extends the growing season by a two or three months in spring and autumn, allowing you to grow veg all year round if you choose. What's more, tender flowers and crops such as aubergines and peppers will thrive in a greenhouse, whereas results will always be limited if you try to grow these plants outside. It will be much easier to propagate your own seedlings, root cuttings and perform countless other tasks that can save you money in the garden.

To get the very best results from your greenhouse, however, it's worth investing time at the outset in selecting the correct location for it, hence it falls to the garden designer to give it some careful consideration.

You don't normally need planning permission to build a greenhouse, but do check this if you live in a conservation area, or if your house is listed. Some councils will also want to know if you plan to build a lean-to greenhouse against a property.

If possible, avoid siting the greenhouse near to boundary walls, public pathways or roads. It's a sad fact that not all passers-by will respect your property, so it's well worth keeping your investment more than a stone's throw away from any potential harm. If your garden opens on to a busy street, consider using plastic for your glazing.

Ideally you should choose a spot that means the ridge

of your greenhouse design will run from east to west. This gives you the advantage of having the whole length of the greenhouse facing the southward sun. This keeps it extra warm in spring and autumn, when your plants are most in need of the extra heat. And in summer, if it gets too hot (which it invariably will) you'll only need to install blinds or organise shading down one side.

Light is obviously a key factor to consider when siting a greenhouse, so avoid placing it in the shade of trees, buildings, large shrubs and garden walls. Bear in mind that the last thing you want is to be cleaning leaves, bird

Scale and style

As with any design challenge, choosing or building the right garden structure requires careful attention to the existing context. Something too large will overwhelm a small garden, while too modest a project will look silly in an otherwise grand design. Matching the style is also important, but given the huge choice presented by garden centres and internet retailers it isn't hard to find something suitable.

droppings and other mess off the roof every day! Also avoid placing your greenhouse at the bottom of a dip or slope, as these positions can mean the temperature inside the house is dramatically reduced – in winter it may even be in a frost pocket.

The next consideration is that you'll probably want a supply of electricity and water to the greenhouse. This usually means it will need to be near your house or garage. The option of having electric lights, heaters and automatic ventilation in your greenhouse can make all the difference to the pleasure you get from using it; and automatic, tap-fed watering systems are a real boon if you're a busy gardener. You'll probably want to set up guttering around the house that feeds into water butts too, as rainwater is wonderful on established crops. But for seedlings it's best to use tap water, as this can help you to avoid fungal diseases such as damping off that can kill whole trays of vulnerable plants overnight.

The other main advantage of having the greenhouse close to your home is that it makes it much easier for you to pop out in the evening and grab some tomatoes, cucumbers and lettuce for dinner! Freshly picked veg always tastes best, so it's a real treat to have food on your plate within minutes of it being harvested.

Another important thing to bear in mind when choosing a site is that it's really handy to be able to walk all the way around the exterior of your greenhouse. Whether

you're cleaning it, replacing an odd panel of glass, or you simply want to grow beans or other climbers up the sides to create a little extra shade, you'll be glad you left yourself this extra room. Ideally aim to have the space to wheel a barrow all around the greenhouse. And if you want cold frames or a compost store right next to the house, leave space around these too.

Once the position is finalised you can create a good solid base for the greenhouse. Mark out the edges of the site with pegs and string. A builder's square can be used to check that the corners are at sharp right angles. Even a small mistake at this stage can create huge problems further down the line, so ensure that the groundwork is completely accurate.

Thoroughly dig over the area to remove all weeds, then dig a footing around the perimeter 150mm wide and deep. Compact the soil and use a spirit level to ensure that the base of the trench is completely level. Fill this trench with a foundation mix of concrete, which can be either one part cement, 2.5 parts sharp sand and 3.5 parts 20mm gravel, or one part cement and five parts all-in ballast. Smooth and level the concrete as you go, then leave it for 48 hours to set hard. Finally, add one or two courses of bricks around the perimeter, on top of which your greenhouse frame will sit. This foundation can add years of life to the structure and is recommended by many greenhouse suppliers.

Cold frames

If you aim to use your greenhouse regularly, then you'll probably want to have a cold frame alongside to make the most of it. The latter is rather like a mini greenhouse (they're usually only up to a metre tall) with wooden or glass sides and an opening glass lid.

Cold frames provide a sort of halfway house and are often used to 'harden off' plants that have been reared in the sheltered environment of the greenhouse. Being kept in the cold frame for a week or two helps them acclimatise to being grown outside, and they can then be planted out in their permanent positions. You can keep the lid of the frame up in the warmth of the day and close it at night to offer your plants extra protection. Plants that aren't hardened off in this way can die or suffer from stunted growth from the shock of the temperature change as a result of going from a warm greenhouse straight into the garden, where nights can be very cold.

Cold frames are also useful for growing-on rooted cuttings and for encouraging flowering plants such as bulbs grown in pots to bloom earlier, thus giving you a longer season of interest. You can also use frames to grow plants such as cucumbers and melons that appreciate the extra shelter offered by the glass, and enjoy the relatively humid conditions inside.

It's relatively easy to make a cold frame if you can get your hands on some old window frames. The ones to look out for are hinged casement designs still in their frames. You can often see these in skips, at car boot sales or even at your council dump. Use planks of wood to make the

back and sides of the frame, while the windows can be used to make the opening top. Ideally frames should be positioned so that they face the sun and slope downwards from the back to the front. This allows water to run off and gives the plants inside the best possible light.

Polytunnels

If you have a very large garden and you're keen to grow lots of vegetables, then another option well worth considering is a polytunnel. While these polythene-covered structures obviously aren't as attractive as a greenhouse, they're relatively inexpensive, they don't take long to erect and they can protect a huge range of crops from planting right up to maturity.

Choose a position near to a water supply if you can, as you'll need a lot of it. Ideally run the tunnel so that the longest side runs from north to south, and choose a model that has as much ventilation as possible. It can get very humid under a layer of plastic, and this can lead to fungal diseases that can severely affect crops like tomatoes, peppers and aubergines.

On the plus side, a polytunnel stays warm for much longer than a greenhouse due to the sheer volume of air inside its large frame. This means your plants won't suffer from huge heat fluctuations on cloudless days when it's baking while the sun is shining but very cool at night.

All the extra space in a polytunnel means that you can easily grow grapes, exotic fruit and larger plants that would take up too much room in the average greenhouse. If you insulate your polytunnel with bubble wrap it's possible to keep it frost-free during the winter, meaning you could even grow citrus fruit, tender flowers and other cold-hating crops.

A polytunnel is only a semi-permanent structure, so you'll need to replace the polythene cover every four to seven years on average. But this can be an advantage in itself, as you can then move the tunnel to a different position in the garden and don't have to worry so much about the possibility of pests and diseases building up in the soil, or depleting certain nutrients from it by growing the same crop in the same space year after year.

If you're intending to keep the tunnel in the same site, however, it's best to practise crop rotation. This simply involves dividing up the areas inside the tunnel and using each one to grow a different type of plant, then literally 'rotating' your plan each year. For example, an area that had brassicas such as broccoli one year would have tomatoes and peppers the following year, followed by carrots and root veg, and then peas and beans.

Seating

Busy gardeners often find it hard to sit still when surrounded by all that growth and potential, but it's important to make the most of your hard work and take a little time to sit and observe. If nothing else, a few well-positioned seats and benches will keep guests out of the way while you get on with your work. They can also be highly decorative features, worthy of occupying a prime spot at the end of a long lawn or pathway.

There's certainly no shortage of garden seating available to buy, but this is very much a case of 'buyer beware'. While you may well pick up some good deals if you know what to look for, far too many offerings are constructed from low-quality softwood held together with cheap fixings. This is a shame, as they'll only last a few years and will very quickly look tatty and unloved. Such purchases are a false economy too, as by saving up for a more expensive, properly constructed item you'll be investing in something that will last several times longer, and look much smarter too.

Seating is also an area in which you can let your creativity loose and construct something of your own design. As the final aim is so simple (a flat surface to sit on, at roughly the right height from the ground) there are countless ways to achieve a useful result. Two supports made from brickwork, timber, stone, old

barrels or whatever takes your fancy, topped with solid timber, gives the most basic but practical bench seat. Explore car boot sales and reclamation yards for materials that inspire you.

An arbour is a more imposing form of seating, usually enclosed to some extent at the back and on either side to give a sense of seclusion and privacy. As with any vertical structure this offers great scope for climbing plants.

Fences and gates

One of the most common features of UK gardens is timber fencing; it's a relatively inexpensive, reasonably long-lasting way to create a boundary that offers privacy as well as pretty good security. It's considered neighbourly to assemble a fence so that any structural elements, such as arris rails, are facing inwards, so that the cleaner face is presented to the outside world.

Whose fence is it?

Most fencing runs along boundaries between one garden and the next, and who owns a particular fence is often the cause of some confusion, not to mention argument, between neighbours. While you may have heard that you own the fence on the left as you look from the house down the garden, you're perhaps just as likely to be under the impression that you own the fence on the right. This is just as true of boundary walls and hedges, and the truth is that there's no hard and fast rule to clear up the confusion.

The most foolproof solution is to check the deeds of your house – if you don't have a copy you should be able to download one for a small fee from the Land Registry website. Many plans, though not all, will be marked with information regarding who's responsible for each boundary.

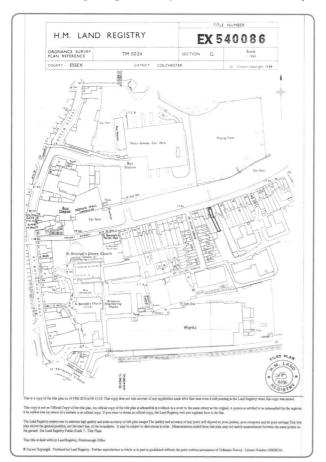

If you can't find out this way then the best thing is just to discuss it openly with your neighbours and see what they think. Often the owner of a boundary fence is simply regarded as he who last renovated it. If no decision is forthcoming, consider sharing any repair and maintenance costs half and half.

Fencing basics

There are many types of fencing panel available to buy, but most of them come in heights of around 1,200, 1,500 or 1,800mm. The standard width of one fence panel is 1,830mm, which corresponds to the old Imperial six feet. The price will depend heavily on the construction method and the timber used, and will often be a direct guide to how long the panel will last. A good strong fence, well-maintained, can last 15 years or more.

The structure of a solid timber fence is straightforward. Vertical timber or concrete posts are either driven into the soil, set in concrete or held in place by metal 'feet'. Attached to these are the timber fence panels. Getting a fence looking good is less straightforward, however. Such a long line of essentially straight timber elements must be carefully aligned, as any deviation in their course is clearly visible.

Marking out a fence

The key to making a fence look good is firstly to get all of the posts in a straight line, and secondly to make sure they're vertical. The first part is easy to achieve if you do your preparation properly. Generally speaking you'll know exactly where the fence should start and end; often this is at a certain point on the wall of the house, and on the boundary line at the far end of the garden. At each of these points set a fence post firmly into the ground, using whatever method you prefer (see below), and tie a piece of string tightly between them. This string gives a good line to which you can work – every panel should be parallel with it and each post should just about touch it.

Setting fence posts in place

There are two options when erecting fence posts, and the one you choose will affect the strength and lifespan of the whole construction. Perhaps the most common approach is to dig a hole for each post, then drop the post into place and concrete the base into position. The depth of the hole depends on the height of the post above ground; up to a metre high requires just 400mm, while 1–2m needs a hole some 700mm deep. The hole does not need to be wide – just 100mm wider than the post is fine.

Line the bottom of the hole with 100mm of broken bricks or stones to provide a firm, free-draining base. Drop in the post and ram down the stones below. A little more hardcore dropped down the sides will help to hold the post in place – check now that it's vertical in both directions. Hammer temporary supports diagonally into the ground and screw them to the post to make sure it doesn't move, then pour your concrete into the hole. Slope the top of the

concrete from the post outwards, so that water is shed away from the fence. Leave for a week to set hard. This method is best for concrete fence posts as there's no danger of them rotting, but can also be used for timber ones provided they're pressure treated.

The other method of installation requires special metal feet to be set in the ground, into which the posts are fixed. Some designs have a spiked base and are simply hammered vertically into the soil. Others are designed to be set into a pad of concrete. Either way they have the advantage of allowing you to change the post should it start to rot, but the spiked versions in particular are less strong than proper concrete footings.

Attaching panels to posts

Some fence posts – most commonly the pre-cast concrete ones – are H-shaped in cross section, which allows you to simply slot the panels into the grooves. Square-section posts can have the panels screwed directly to them, but you can also buy metal fittings that screw to the post and make the job of attaching the panel slightly easier.

Maintaining timber

Some types of timber will last for years without any attention, while others (usually the cheaper ones) will need more regular care to keep them looking good. Most garden structures need to be worked on in situ, so choose a fine dry day at the end of summer to renovate them and keep the winter weather at bay. Start by rubbing them down with sandpaper or wire wool, then giving one or two coats of timber preservative or paint as appropriate.

Types of fence panel

LAP
A frame of timber, with an infill of thin planks set so that each one overlaps the next. Square-, feather- or wavy-edged wood can be used, but the overlap should be a minimum of 20mm to ensure that the boards don't pop out of place. Vertical and horizontal lap panels are available, the difference being the direction in which the planks run.

INTERWOVEN
Inexpensive and popular, interwoven panels have horizontal strips of wood woven between vertical boards. Chinks between the strips allow limited visibility, so not the best choice for a private garden.

CLOSEBOARD
The most solid of timber fence constructions, closeboard panels are often assembled on site from arris rails (running horizontally between the posts) and vertical 100–150mm-wide boards.

Installing a fence
With the first and last fence posts in place as described above, start from one end and fix your first panel in place. Timber panels are best used just a few centimetres off the ground to avoid the damp, so rest them on a couple of bricks while you fix them in place. Ensure the panel is horizontal with a spirit level (you can knock one of the bricks into the soil to help with this) and that it exactly follows the string line tied between the posts.

When you're happy with the position, fix the second fence post in place so that it abuts the panel and fix the two together, again checking your verticals in all directions. Continue in this way down the garden until all the panels and posts are in place. It's unlikely that the length of your fence will be an exact multiple of the length of a panel, so you may have to cut the final panel down, as described below.

Cutting a fence panel to length
There may come a time when you need to insert a fence panel into a gap that's an awkward size or shape. If you're building your fence from scratch then you can allow for this, but if you're using ready-made panels, as most people now do, it's possible to cut one down to size if you know how. The trick is to make a new frame to hold the cladding in place, and to do this before you make any cuts to resize the panel. This way you don't end up with a bundle of flapping planks that are only supported at one end. Use two lengths of strong timber batten, one screwed to either side of the fence in the correct position to act as the 'end' of the panel. You shouldn't have to screw every piece of the cladding to these if you make sure you screw them tightly to each other. When they're in place, use a hand saw to cut carefully down the outside of the new batten strips to remove the unwanted part of the panel.

Other types of fencing

There are many other ways of making fencing, using a variety of materials. Some offer less privacy than a line of full-height panels, but may well be suited to divisions within the garden – perhaps around a children's play area or a vegetable patch.

Trellis

Made from a grid of narrow timber battens, trellis has an open structure that's ideal for creating soft, visually-pleasing divisions within a garden. It's also a very good way to add extra height to an existing fence; two-foot trellis panels are often used to top four-foot lap or closeboard fence panels. The open structure allows views through the trellis, and is also ideal for training climbing plants. A trellis boundary is a good security measure, as it acts as an obstruction but is too weak to be safely climbed. There are now quite a few decorative alternatives to the basic design, with rustic poles, bamboo or even lengths of rope replacing the inner timbers.

Chain link or wire

Rather a utilitarian approach, wire fences don't provide privacy and aren't the most attractive of features. They do provide some security if tall enough, but in gardens they're much more commonly used as a low division between plots.

Chain link is a strong mesh of wires, easy to use and relatively inexpensive. All types of wire fencing require strong upright posts, as the wire must be pulled very taught during installation.

Wattles

These traditional panels have been made for centuries out of local materials. They're literally woven from strips of tough but flexible bark and thin branches (very often hazel), wound around vertical stakes that can be pushed into the ground. They're full of rustic charm, just the thing for a country cottage or for edging an ornamental kitchen garden.

Paling

Not as common a sight as it once was, paling is bought as a roll and consists of irregular stakes (usually chestnut) tied to three lengths of horizontal wire. Paling must be supported by strong posts positioned every 1,800mm or so.

Picket fencing

Similar to paling, a picket fence has vertical timber elements spaced quite widely and nailed to horizontal supports. It differs from paling in that the horizontal elements are also made from timber – two or three depending on the height of the fence. Again, sturdy vertical posts are required as supports.

Tree houses

Not, perhaps, the most common addition to a garden, a tree house would nonetheless be high on the list of must-haves if the whole family were involved in the design process. There's something about them that never fails to make people stop and smile – perhaps we have some innate genetic memory of living in the treetops, or maybe it's just the fond recollection of the adventures we had as kids.

Whatever the reason behind the appeal, it's surely something we should give in to more often! If you have the right tree then a tree house can be more than just a play area for the kids. It could be a viewing platform if you're surrounded by countryside, or it could be a dining room or even a spare bedroom in good weather.

If you don't have any large trees, it's possible to build around a smaller tree by using timber posts to support the frame. Either way it's important to have a strong frame of horizontal timbers in place before you start building the floor or walls.

Don't forget that the planning authorities may well object if you build something that looks too professional, or too permanent. Neighbours should also be considered, as nobody wants next door's kids staring in through their bedroom window or down into their garden.

GARDEN LANDSCAPING

PONDS AND
WATER FEATURES

Ponds and water features

Anyone interested in wildlife, or who wants to create a garden with additional areas of interest, should think seriously about including water amongst their design tools.

The earliest gardens were created in the Middle East over 2,500 years ago (some say even earlier – 5,000 years or more). They were enclosed, private paradises where man had dominion over nature, and water consistently played a central role. It's varied potential to reflect images or shadows, to bounce light, to make restful noises and to cool the surrounding area are still used in modern design, and you might even ask if gardens have really developed very much since that time.

Building a pond, particularly a large or formal construction, takes quite a bit of work and a little regular maintenance. Get the conditions right, however, and it should look after itself through much of the year. Fountains, streams and waterfalls can all be added later (or indeed can exist as elements on their own), and you'll have a whole new range of plants with which to experiment. Ponds often become a focal point, drawing garden visitors closer and inviting relaxation and quiet contemplation. If you have the space it's really worth trying to include some kind of water feature in your design.

Pond liners

Perhaps the most important element of any pond, liners come in a variety of shapes and sizes. It pays to choose the right one first time, as mistakes are very difficult to rectify later! Generally speaking you need to choose between a preformed, rigid plastic shell and a flexible PVC or butyl membrane. You can also line ponds with concrete, or even 'puddled' clay, but these methods are no longer common. The most important things to consider when shopping for a liner are your method of construction and your end visual intention.

If you want a natural-looking pond with irregular, wavy edges then a flexible liner is probably the best choice. This will allow you to shape the edges however you wish, and will give the least artificial appearance. You can buy rigid liners designed to look irregular and natural, but somehow they never quite succeed. They do often incorporate planting ledges however, and may be easier for a novice to install.

If your pond is a formal, geometric shape then rigid liners become a much better proposition. You can buy them ready-made to the correct size and depth, saving the hassle of folding a flexible liner carefully to make square corners, or a perfectly circular edge. Either style can be used in an excavated or raised pond.

Building a pond

1 Use a hosepipe or a line of sand to mark out the edges of your pond on the ground. If you're using a rigid liner you'll need to transfer the exact shape to the ground; with a flexible liner you can be more creative, but avoid tight corners as they're hard to work with.

2 Remove the turf and dig out the soil to the required depth. Shape the edges of the pond as you dig to the match the shape of your rigid liner, or into a natural slope if you're using flexible material. Either way you can leave planting shelves along the edges if required.

3 Remove any sharp stones and anything else that might puncture your liner. Line the excavation with an underlay of geotextile membrane or a 25mm layer of soft sand, then lay the liner in place. Backfill any gaps around a rigid liner with sand or soil.

4 Don't cut off any excess flexible liner until the pond is full, as it may shift and settle under the weight of the water. When the pond is full, trim the liner, install any edging you intend to use and then start adding plants. Let the water stand for a few weeks before adding fish.

Edging a pond

The edge of a pond is often the most visible part, yet it's all too often treated as an afterthought. The principal function of pond edging is to disguise the liner – you don't want to see folds of butyl membrane or a hard shoulder of plastic. Depending on the style of your pond, the edging may help it stand out or blend into its surroundings; to look natural, or formal and controlled. It's the frame within which the rest of the feature exists, and as such can set the tone for the whole pond.

Paving

One of the simplest and longest-lasting options, paving provides a firm boundary and prevents any erosion of the banks. Clear and level an area of surrounding ground large enough to accommodate the pavers. Excavate the soil to a depth of 50mm and lay your paving on to a strong mortar mix. Allow the pavers to overhang the edge of the pond by a few centimetres and this will help to conceal the liner if the water level drops slightly. Be careful not to drop any mortar into the pond, as it will affect the water chemistry drastically.

Bricks can certainly be used as a paved edging, and are particularly good for following gently curved lines. They'll need their joints pointing, and you may want to buy engineering bricks as they'll withstand the wet conditions better.

An artificial beach

A great option for the wildlife garden, this provides a gentle slope that can be used by small animals to gain access to the water. You need to build in this slope at the excavation stage, then lay a flexible liner in place and cover this with pebbles or stones in a mixture of sizes. Spread the stones a little way bellow the water line, or even right into the bottom of the pool if the design allows. A few plants mixed in with the stones can add to the natural feel.

Plants and grass

The objective here is to give the illusion of a natural pond or riverbank, so it works best if you can conceal any artificial elements such as cables, pipework and, of course, the liner. You can bring the lawn right up to the edge of the water, but it's difficult to hide the liner this way. Spreading and trailing plants are the solution – allow them to grow right down into the water and mix with taller varieties to give a balanced effect. Use nectar-rich plants such as wild flowers to attract a range of insects and to make your feature as busy and diverse as possible. Don't forget about the changing seasons – include as many evergreen foliage plants as you have room for to give winter interest.

Plants to edge your pond

Try a combination of the following plants as a natural edging choice. They'll grow in shallow water and creep on to the land, giving a seamless transition from pond to garden.

■ **Marsh marigold (Caltha palustris)**
Bright yellow buttercup-like flowers in early spring. Glossy green leaves and very easy to grow.

■ **Water mint (Mentha aquatica)**
Like any mint this can spread rapidly. The trick to controlling it is to grow it in a basket and trim the leaves and any emerging roots regularly. Lavender-coloured flowers appear in the summer.

■ **Bowles' golden sedge (Carex elata 'Aurea')**
Yellow grassy foliage that grows to about 50cm high. Very eye-catching.

■ **Monkey flower (Mimulus luteus)**
The yellow flowers have attractive red blotches on the petals. Grows to about 20cm high.

■ ***Houttuynia cordata***
White flowers are borne on heart-shaped green foliage, which spreads easily. Try the variety 'Chameleon' for its red, gold and green leaves.

■ **Water forget-me-not (Myosotis scorpioides)**
Creeping and free-flowering all summer, the blooms are very much like the pink garden forget-me-not.

■ **Soft rush (Juncus effusus)**
A good choice for a wildlife pond. The rush grows up to 60cm in height and self-seeds to spread.

■ **Brooklime (Veronica beccabunga)**
Glossy creeping foliage with bright blue, white-centred flowers in summer.

Encouraging wildlife

If you want a really natural pond with plenty of diverse wildlife, the most important thing to do is to avoid adding fish. Goldfish and other pond favourites are aggressively carnivorous and will devour the eggs and larvae of most other pond inhabitants.

Make sure you add plenty of plant material around the edges of the pond so that amphibians, non-aquatic insects, birds and mammals all feel protected when they come to the water's edge. If you're building a new pond, introduce a bucket of silt from an established one. This will contain many small creatures that will help to speed-up the colonisation process. Make sure there's enough vegetation beneath the pond's surface, on which aquatic insects can lay their eggs. Oxygenating plants are ideal, as are water lilies and anything with a vigorous aquatic root systems.

Look for native plants when stocking your pond, as it's with these that our native creatures will feel most at home. Rather than aiming for an ultra-clean pool, it's no bad thing if you allow a layer of silt to build up in the depths. Many bugs will burrow into this for food and shelter. Lastly, be patient! If your pond provides the right conditions then wildlife will find you in time.

Raised ponds

If you're not intent on creating a natural-looking garden then a raised pond may well be worth considering. You'll avoid all the strenuous excavations, and the final water surface will be closer to eye level, allowing you to better appreciate the plants and animals within. It is also a great way to add seating to your garden – imagine sitting on the paved edge of a raised brick pond, watching the fish and trailing your fingers in the water.

Raising a pond also makes it more of a centrepiece, perhaps becoming the visual focus of the garden. It can work well in a formal context where regular geometric lines stand out against the softer surroundings of lawn or borders. You can choose materials to suit your garden; rendered concrete is strong and relatively easy to use, brickwork offers a softer look, while weathered stone or even railway sleepers will work well with more natural design schemes.

One drawback is that the water is above ground level, and so doesn't benefit from the insulation provided by surrounding soil. This means water temperatures will fluctuate more quickly, which is bad news for fish if you choose to keep them. You can mitigate this problem by having the pond partly raised and partly sunken, giving fish a deeper refuge into which they can retreat in a hot summer or cold winter.

Pond pumps

If you want to include an artificial filtration system, a fountain, waterfall or any other kind of moving water, then a pond pump is essential. Be careful to choose the right size and type, though, as there are many available, each with its own abilities and purpose. Generally speaking the type of pump that sits under the water is the cheaper option, not to mention being hidden from view and almost completely quiet. Non-submersible pumps are also available, but as they require separate housing they're often only used in larger, more professional installations.

The maximum output of the pump, measured in litres per hour, will decide its suitability for your application. Remember that the figures given by manufacturers are likely to be achievable only in ideal test conditions. In reality they may be a little ambitious. It's a good idea to oversize your pump by around 20% for this reason.

If your pump is required to run a filtration system, you should aim to move the entire volume of your pond once every hour. In other words, if you have a 5,000-litre pond you need a pump that can move 5,000 litres per hour. To calculate your pond volume, multiply the average length by the average width, then by the average depth (all in metres). Multiply the result by 1,000 to get the volume in litres.

For waterfalls, streams and fountains the required pump output depends entirely on the amount of water you want to move. A small fountain will require very little, while a rushing stream will require a great deal more. Ask for advice from your pump supplier in this situation; they'll need to know the length of the pipework and the height to which the water will be lifted (known as the 'head').

Fountains

The easiest way to bring movement to a water feature is to install a fountain. All that's required is a suitable power supply and a submersible pump. A pipe runs from the pump to just above the surface of the pond, and water is shot upwards out of this.

The pattern or dispersal of the water can be controlled by attaching different nozzles to the pipe, and many fountain pumps come with a range of options. Common choices include single, double and triple-layer sprinklers, bell-shaped sprays and a single bubbling column. All are great for breaking up the surface of the water to improve the oxygen content (important for fish, especially in hot weather) and for attracting wildlife – birds in particular.

Wall fountains

If you lack space in your garden, or if you just want a simple way to include moving water without digging a full-scale pond, then a wall fountain may be for you. Big on impact but with a small footprint, wall fountains consist of some form of water reservoir (perhaps a trough or sink) with a spout in the wall above. A pump in the bottom of the reservoir provides water to the spout via a hidden pipe inside or behind the wall, and the result is a happy little trickle of water and some very relaxing sounds. Depending on the size of the reservoir you may be able to add plants, or even a few small fish.

131

Waterfalls and streams

Whether you prefer a natural-looking flow of water, meandering along a route of natural stone, or the more artificial look of a brick-lined rill or steel-spouted waterfall, moving water is a great addition to all kinds of garden design. It fascinates children, attracts wildlife and even conceals background noise.

Most such projects are simple in their design – you need a water reservoir at the lower end (often this job is performed by a garden pond), with a pump suitably sized to move enough water the required height and distance, and a downhill route for the water to follow. The most challenging part of the installation is making sure none of the water escapes from the route, as this will quickly empty your reservoir. If you don't have a pond already you can create a reservoir specifically for the purpose.

Calculating flow

Wider streams and waterfalls need more water moving through them than narrow ones. To find out how great a flow you need, measure the average width in centimetres and multiply by 100. This is the required flow in litres per hour. Remember, the higher the head, the lower the flow rate of the pump will be.

Light and water

While we'll cover the practicalities of outdoor electrics in Chapter 7, it's worth mentioning underwater lighting here too. Pond lights come in a range of shapes and sizes, allowing plenty of scope for creativity. Some units cast light upwards from the base of the pond, silhouetting aquatic plants and fish to give you a fascinating insight into life below the surface. Others float on the surface to illuminate the pond margins and to cast reflections on the surface of the water.

Moving water is a particularly good subject for lighting, as the ripples and splashes diffuse the light and throw dancing patterns on to nearby surfaces. Some styles of light can be attached to the spout of a fountain, lighting the spray from within, while a backlit waterfall will bring the garden to life after dark.

Some manufacturers supply their lights with a variety of coloured lenses, giving you a choice of lighting effects from classically elegant to downright eerie. Amber light works well with water, but good designers are careful not to overuse coloured lighting – a touch of colour can be breathtaking, but use too much and you'll spoil the effect.

The same can be said of light in general; the most effective installations use light sparingly, drawing the eye to a statue or architectural plant. Some units are so stylish that they're worth making a feature of in themselves. Other lamps, less visually appealing, are designed to be hidden amongst planting where their light will pick out the shapes of foliage in the water. Remember that while lighting can transform your pond by night, you don't want the equipment to detract from the pond by day. Thoughtful positioning is key.

Building a waterfall or stream

1 Shape the soil along the route of your watercourse into a series of shallows and drops, aiming to make it look as natural as possible. If you can't make use of a natural slope, build one up using soil, but make sure you compact it well.

2 Run the supply pipe from the pump up one side of the route of the stream to the 'source', bedding the pipe into the soil or sand as much as possible. Cover the soil with a geotextile fabric, or a layer of soft sand to protect the liner.

3 Cover the route with a single strip of flexible pond liner, leaving some excess at each side. Turn on the water flow to ensure none escapes off the sides of the liner. Lastly cover the liner with suitably shaped flat rocks, stones and gravel.

4 Large or sharply pointed rocks should be sat on more geotextile membrane to protect the liner, and may need a blob of mortar to hold them in place. Add plants along the route of the water so they overhang the flow.

Pond filtration

While a natural or wildlife pond should be a well-balanced ecosystem and will require only occasional intervention, sometimes an artificial system is also required to keep the water clean and clear. This is especially true if you keep fish, as they tend to create much more waste and pollution than a typical garden pond can deal with.

A good standard filter consists of two stages. The first has water passing through a filter medium, often a course sponge or foam. This physically blocks the passage of large, solid pieces of dirt, and is the part of the filter that most often needs to be removed and cleaned. The second stage is biological, which means it has a large surface area (often provided by brushes, porous stones etc) upon which grows a colony of beneficial bacteria. These helpful microorganisms digest the harmful pollutants in the pond water, breaking them down into more benign components. The bacteria will build up naturally over time, and you should avoid washing out the biological stage of the filter with chlorinated water, which will greatly reduce their numbers.

More advanced filters may also have a third stage which passes the water past an intense ultraviolet bulb. This kills algal cells and prevents the greening of water so commonly seen in warm weather.

Filters are often installed out of the water to allow for easy inspection and maintenance. This can affect the look of the pond, however, so you might want to consider concealing your equipment behind a screen or amongst plants.

Despite the benefits of artificial filtration, there are plenty of people who prefer a less intrusive approach. So-called vegetable filters use the natural ability of plants to draw pollutants from the water – in fact the plants use these as food. By populating your pond with hungry, fast-growing varieties and by quickly removing any dead or dying plant matter you can keep a pond remarkably clear. This is a slow-acting option, however, and is not the best choice for a well-stocked fish pond.

Dealing with algae

Surely the most prevalent problem in garden ponds is green water caused by an excess of algae. While these tiny floating organisms are rarely harmful to the pond or its inhabitants, their overall effect is far from attractive and pea-green water doesn't help you to observe the fish or wildlife within.

Algae can be divided into two categories: suspended floating cells, which cause green murky water; and filamentous algae such as blanket weed, which fill the pond with a thick carpet-like growth. The simplest method of control is to create a balanced environment that doesn't allow algae to develop freely. Submerged plants will devour nutrients, while floating plants will provide shade and deprive algae of the light required for growth. Using this system, and unless you introduce fish, you may experience a few algal 'blooms', but the water should gradually become clear and stable.

Making a vegetable filter

1 Place a large container in the pond so that the rim lies some 50mm below the surface. Line the base with bricks or large rocks to weigh it down.

2 Fill a strong net or string bag with coarse, clean gravel and tie it closed. Place this into the container so that it lies just below the surface of the water.

3 Thread watercress, or seedlings of other fast-growing aquatics, through the net and bed their roots gently into the gravel. All their nutrients will come from the pond.

4 As the plants grow to fill the available space, use scissors to chop away sections of the foliage. If they fail to regrow simply introduce more seedlings.

Floating plants

Surely the easiest of additions to the garden pond, free-floating plants can simply be bought from aquatics centres, brought home and dropped into the water. Their dangling roots will takes excess nutrients from the water, while the shade they cast will make life hard for algae while protecting any fish from predators such as herons. They can be very fast-growing, however, and there are some invasive foreign species, including fairy moss *(Azolla filiculoides)* and water chestnut *(Trapa natans)* that must be avoided at all costs. Some of the best options include:

■ Frogbit *(Hydrocharis morsus-ranae)*

A British native, frogbit is not showy but does have small, shiny, lily-pad shaped leaves and pleasant white flowers. It's a good option for smaller, self-contained water features.

■ Water hyacinth *(Eichhornia crassipes)*

The most popular floater in UK ponds, the water hyacinth has luxurious shiny foliage with bulbous bases containing natural flotation chambers. A central flower spike covered in numerous pink to purple flowers gives the plant its common name.

■ Water lettuce *(Pistia stratiotes)*

Not a real lettuce, of course, but the colour, shape and texture of the foliage do look remarkably similar.

Maintaining a pond

For many would-be pond owners, the one thing that puts them off is the thought of maintenance. Battling green water, cutting back plants, removing blanket weed, it can all seem a little intimidating. However, as long as you take a few precautions and give it some light but regular TLC your pond should naturally regulate itself.

Preparation is key: it's at the planning and installation stage that many pond projects are made or broken. Over-stocking, inadequate filtration or overly invasive plants will all lead to problems further down the line. To minimise your workload try to give your pond the best start possible. Make sure fish ponds have a filtration system that can handle the water volume from day one – it's much harder for a filter to achieve good water quality if it's added as an afterthought to an already filthy pond. Plant native, rather than foreign species, as they'll settle more comfortably and will need less regular attention. Introduce fish gradually over a period of weeks to give your system a chance to adapt. Remember that some fish species can grow to an impressive size, so always consider their adult proportions when stocking your pond.

Once the pond is correctly set up you'll simply need to carry out a straightforward but regular programme of maintenance according to the type of pond and the time of year.

Spring

Clean out the pump and filter early in the spring to get the filtration system up and running before the weather, and the metabolism of pond inhabitants, picks up. If you want to replant the margins now is your chance. New plants will have plenty of time to establish before the onset of winter. Lift and divide those plants that have spread out too much, and start feeding your fish if they're active.

Summer

Pond plants should need relatively little attention. Feed them with an aquatic fertiliser and tidy up any excess growth, but otherwise leave them to their own devices. For serious fishponds, however, this is a busy time of year. You must check nitrite, ammonia, pH and nitrate levels regularly, and ideally change up to 20% of the pond water every couple of weeks. Hoover up any build-up of sludge on the pond floor using a special pond vacuum.

Autumn

Falling leaves are the biggest problem at this time of year. Either scoop them out with a fishing net, or else net the whole pond to prevent them from falling into the water. Towards the end of the season life in the pond will be slow; this is the perfect time to carry out any repairs or construction. If your pond is in really poor shape, this is the best time to perform a complete clean out.

Winter

The main task in winter is seeing the pond and its inhabitants through the cold weather. If you have fish you must try and keep at least part of the surface free from ice. Otherwise it's a fairly quite time; take advantage of this by inspecting your pond and coming up with ideas to improve the design, or new plants to install.

Cleaning your pond

You should only clean your pond out completely if you have serious water quality problems. This is best done at the end of autumn, or failing that at the beginning of spring, when the plant and animal life is dormant. Lift out any plants in containers and drain out all the water. Remove all the sludge and debris, gently scrubbing the liner clean of algae before refilling with tap water. A dechlorinator may help the water chemistry to return to normal more quickly.

Pumps and filters should be removed and thoroughly cleaned at the same time. Try and get into a routine of cleaning these every week or so and you'll notice the difference in water quality. Remove and rinse out the filter media and wash out the chamber. You should use some of the old pond water, or rainwater if you have a water butt, as chlorinated water can kill the helpful bacteria that will be growing in your filter.

Repairing a leaking pond

There are many reasons why the level of water in your pond might start to drop. In summer, evaporation can lead to quite serious water loss and there's little you can do to prevent this. If the drop seems more sudden, however, it's possible there's a leak somewhere in the system. Make sure any fountains aren't splashing water out of the pond, and that streams or waterfalls aren't losing water somewhere along their length (damp ground nearby is a giveaway). Next check all pipework associated with these same features, and with your filtration system if you have one. If all seams fine, and particularly if the drop in your water level always stops at the same point, then it's likely the pond liner has a leak.

Most such leaks can be fixed, but the technique varies according to the type of pond.

CONCRETE LINERS

Lower the water level to just below the crack. If it's just a fine crack, scrub the surface and paint it with two of three layers of sealant. If the damage is wider, chisel out any loose material to leave a gap around 20–30mm wide. Fill with fresh concrete, leave for a week to set hard, and then refill the pond.

FLEXIBLE PVC LINERS

Because of their low price, many people opt for PVC liners over butyl ones. Their lightness also makes them useful for quickly-built wildlife ponds, but they're prone to leaks. They have a short lifespan, and although kits exist to fix any small holes or tears you might be better replacing the whole liner with a butyl alternative.

Pond safety

If you have young children you should be careful to control their access to a pond. While the wildlife a pond attracts is in turn fascinating to young children, deep water, slippery edges and electrical equipment all pose risks. It's possible to install a metal grille either above or just below the surface of a pond to stop people from falling into the water. Those few fatal accidents that do occur each year in the UK tend to involve children who are visiting someone else's garden, rather than children who have grown up with a pond and have had its dangers explained to them.

Safety measures should also extend to protecting wildlife – too many hedgehogs and other small mammals fall into ponds while looking for a drink, and then can't climb back out because the artificial liner is so slippery. Make sure you allow a means of escape – a sunken log pinned with one end out of the water is one option, as is a large stone with rough, climbable edges.

FLEXIBLE BUTYL LINERS

Rather more robust than PVC, butyl is strong enough to warrant repairing if it's punctured. Some repair kits will even work under water, but to be on the safe side lower the water level, clean the damaged area thoroughly and stick on the repair patch.

RIGID LINERS

Quality varies greatly with price, and the best method of repair will depend on the construction material. You can try lowering the water level and fixing a waterproof patch over the crack, using strong sealant glue.

GARDEN LANDSCAPING

OUTDOOR ELECTRICS AND LIGHTING

7

Outdoor electrics and lighting

While it was once the case that a householder could do their own electrical installations and repairs, the law now requires most major work to be carried out by what's known as a 'competent person' – essentially a qualified electrician. This means that adding an electrical system to your garden now carries an added expense, but the improved safety aspect is well worth the cost. While you may well feel confident that your own work would be safe, you would doubtless be reassured that any work carried out by a previous installer was up to scratch.

This is no area in which to take chances. Wiring outdoors has the potential to be lethal if incorrectly installed or used. The likelihood of damage or wear and tear to electrical equipment is greater than it is indoors, and the environmental conditions are much less controlled. One obvious concern is the presence of water, both in the ground and falling from the sky, which can obviously lead to electrical safety issues. No wonder, then, that building regulations are now so strict when it comes to outdoor electrics.

What this means, of course, is that your involvement in outdoor electrical projects is limited. You're still legally allowed to repair a damaged cable, switch or socket, or to change fittings such as lamps; but you aren't permitted to install a complete new circuit, or to extend an existing one. Instead your main role is to choose the effects you want your installation to have – and after all, this is the most important part of the process.

One useful way of getting involved with an electrical installation, and perhaps more importantly of keeping the associated costs down, is to do some of the more physical work before your electrician begins. It's quite likely that you'll need to bury under the lawn and flowerbeds one or more supply cables

that run from the consumer unit in the main house or garage to the required site of garden lighting, a shed with a power supply, or a pond with pump and filters. There's very little point paying a skilled electrician his full daily rate to do such basic work, and you can cut his bill drastically by having it ready for him when he arrives.

You may choose to do this preparation work yourself, but if you don't fancy the idea it would still be wise to arrange for a less skilled, less expensive tradesman to quote for the job. The electrician will probably be more than happy to help you decide on the route your wiring should take, and it's well worth consulting him before you dig. He'll also give you instructions regarding the depth of the trench, but 450mm is usually a safe minimum. Once the electrician has the cable in place, and is happy for you to cover it, give it some extra protection by laying a row of old roof tiles or slates over the top. Part backfill the trench, then add a strip of hazard warning tape before filling the trench to ground level.

Outdoor sockets and switches

Thanks to a growing range of weather-resistant fittings, it isn't necessary to position the controls for your exterior electrics inside the house. Instead you can have external switches, perhaps with a remote control, that allow you to do everything from the patio, summer house or elsewhere in the garden. You can also install external sockets to give you the option to add other temporary equipment at a later date. This is a wise addition, well worth considering, and shouldn't add too much to the overall cost.

As the installer will be sure to tell you, sockets and switches should be positioned well off the ground on a wall or a sturdy post. Any cabling that emerges from the ground and runs up to these fittings must be protected by armoured conduit running from the fittings themselves to well below ground level.

Outdoor electrics: the costs

If you want any mains-powered, external electrical devices you'll need to have a circuit installed that begins and ends at your consumer unit (often called a fuse box). The main expense involved with such a project is usually the running of the cables from the fuse box to the devices themselves. Partly this is because of the work involved; it can often require running a new cable quite a distance through the house, then across the garden. This would be time consuming in itself, but add to this the fact that external cables must be buried deep below the ground and you'll see how the work can mount up. What's more, any mains cable used in the garden must be of a special armoured construction, with a spiral of protective steel wrapped around the current-carrying inner wire. This cable isn't cheap, and you may well need plenty of it.

Low-voltage systems

One way of avoiding the effort and cost of a full mains-powered system is to use low-voltage equipment. There are quite a few such lighting systems, but your options when it comes to pond pumps and so on are more limited. Nonetheless, the systems are fairly easy to install, and certainly much safer than mains. They consist of an indoor transformer, which plugs into a socket and reduces the mains voltage before sending it on out into the garden. You'll need a suitable spot to locate the transformer (remember, they can get quite hot and shouldn't be covered while in use), and you may need to drill a hole through an exterior wall to pass the cable into the garden.

As the voltage is no longer at a potentially dangerous level, there's no need to bury the cable along its outdoor route, but that said you still don't want to snag it with your garden fork, so it's a good idea to run it somewhere out of the way, perhaps tacked along a fence.

Low-voltage systems are often supplied with a remote control device, which allows you to turn lights on and off from a distance.

Using an extension lead in the garden

If you don't have the funds to install a dedicated outdoor power supply, one simple way to provide electricity for your electrical garden tools, such as mowers, strimmers and hedge cutters, is to run a long extension lead from a plug socket in the house out into the garden. There's nothing wrong with this idea in principle, but you must observe some important rules to ensure you're working safely.

Firstly, when working outdoors all of your power tools, and the extension lead itself, must be protected by something called a residual current device (RCD). This is a wonderfully simple invention that works on the principle that electrical systems operate via circuits – in other words, the positive supply is twinned with a negative return. The RCD measures the current on both of these simultaneously, and if it measures a difference outside of the range considered safe it will immediately (well, within milliseconds) cut off the power. In practice this means any leak of current to the outside world, such as that which might be caused by a loose connection, or by you cutting the supply cable with your lawn mower, will cause the RCD to trip.

It's quite common to find an RCD already built into your consumer unit, particularly if you already have one or more circuits that supply outbuildings or external mains-powered lighting. Any plug sockets on this circuit will automatically benefit from the protection of the RCD, but it's vital that you make sure you have correctly identified the circuit. Plug into a normal household socket on a non-protected circuit and the RCD can't help you.

A safer way of working is to buy an RCD adapter that can be plugged into any socket, RCD-protected or not, and then provides protection for any extension lead that you plug into it. RCD devices usually have a test button that should cause them to trip. Make sure you press this button each time you plug into the RCD to ensure it's operating correctly.

Another more obvious safety consideration when using extension leads is to ensure that they're kept out of the way of the tools they're supplying. It can be a good habit to work with the lead hooked over your shoulder so it doesn't dangle over your working area. You should also make sure the lead is visible – a black wire laid across longish grass can easily disappear, and you need to know exactly where it is before you cut that grass. A related concern is the potential to trip over wires – dangerous in itself but more so if you're wielding a power tool. Keep excess cabling tidy and pay attention to where you're placing your feet.

One risk not widely acknowledged is that of the cable overheating. This can occur sometimes when a long reel of cable is plugged in without being unwound first, because the passage of current causes the wires to heat up. It's particularly likely in hot, direct sunlight and can result in the whole reel catching fire. Remove the risk by unrolling the whole reel before switching on, and keeping any loops of unused cable out of the sun.

Lastly, the risks mentioned earlier of combining water and electrics are particularly important here – extension leads by their nature have joins at each end, and these have the potential to let in water. Try to keep such connections off the ground, and don't work in damp weather.

Lighting in your garden

There are many ways of using light in your garden, and the effect of your installation will vary according to a number of factors. Whether you want purely ornamental effects, or practical illumination, the type, strength, direction, colour and location of your lights are all important. Lighting not only makes your garden more beautiful, it also adds security and makes outdoor activities safer. What's more, it allows you to enjoy your garden from indoors after dark, and, of course, to extend the hours in which you can make use of your outdoor space to entertain or relax.

Area lighting

The most straightforward proposal is to light an area of the garden so that it can be used safely and comfortably. You could use one large light, but this can often be rather dazzling and leads to harsh shadows. Better to use a number of smaller lights to cast a more even glow – each one is then required to be less intense and won't blind people who chance to look in the wrong direction. Functional lighting, perhaps in a carport or beneath a front porch, needn't be ugly if you choose your equipment wisely.

If you have a passion for dining and entertaining *al fresco*, then a softly-lit patio or deck will have plenty of appeal. Remember that you don't need a great intensity of light – indeed, this could be unwelcoming and might leave you feeling exposed in the comparatively dark surroundings. Aim for a soft even glow rather than the sort of light levels you might need to work by. A good way of having extra control over this is to install a number of different circuits, perhaps with wall lights, recessed floor spots and overhead lighting all working independently of one another, allowing you to play with a variety of combinations. Another excellent idea is to add a dimmer switch to one or more of these circuits, allowing precise control.

Route lighting

One of the most practical uses for outdoor illumination is to light a route from one part of the garden to another. This may be purely functional, such as a line of bulkhead lamps spaced regularly down a passageway to give an even, usable light, or it may be more romantic and ornamental, such as a line of fairy lights strung loosely in tree branches above a winding path. If you want permanent mains lighting, perhaps along a main path down the garden or alongside a driveway, then it will save time and effort if you can get the wiring in place at the same time as installing the paving.

Ornamental lighting effects

UP-LIGHTING

The most easily achieved and frequently implemented of lighting effects, up-lighting has lost none of its impact through overuse. All that's required is a single, directional light source placed below and in front of the target area. It's effective both with natural subject matter such as a canopy of leaves, and with more grand material such as statuary or the underside of a stone archway.

DOWN-LIGHTING

This involves a directional light fitting mounted high on a wall, shining downwards. It's most commonly used on the exterior walls of a building to give a pretty, atmospheric effect and a useful diffuse light in the surrounding area. It can also be used to illuminate a particularly interesting statue or plant from above.

CROSS-LIGHTING

A modern and stylish technique, requiring two separate sources of light. The effect is rather softer than down-lighting as it produces fewer hard shadows. This is a great way of picking out a central ornamental feature in the garden, or perhaps even your front door.

Security lighting

Not the most exciting of additions to a garden, security lamps are nonetheless a very worthwhile idea. They might be switched on and off remotely, like any other light, or they might be automatically triggered by a motion sensor or by a timer. Apart from the potential to deter unwanted guests, such an arrangement can serve to make jobs like putting out the rubbish, or even getting from the car to the house, safer and more comfortable.

Do consider your neighbours if you want to go down this route. Security lighting by its nature is very bright, and nobody wants one shining into their bedroom window on a windy night, when a swinging tree branch activates the motion sensor every few minutes.

Temporary lights

If you don't want to take on the work involved with a full, hard-wired lighting installation, you could instead opt for temporary, battery-powered lights or even candles. There are now many products available that can simply be hung from the branches of a tree or pushed into the ground on stakes. Be aware that the quality of these products can often reflect their non-permanent nature, and try to remember to bring them inside when they're not in use. Drawbacks aside, they're an easy and fun way to jazz-up your garden for a celebration, or perhaps a dinner party *al fresco*.

Solar lighting

One idea that has recently become more practical is that of using solar power to run the lights in your garden. This involves a small solar panel that charges an integral battery through the day, so that after dark this stored power can be used to run one or more lamps. Often these have light sensors included so that they turn themselves on automatically as dusk falls – a useful way of making commonly-used walkways safer after dark.

While such equipment hasn't always been very reliable (or, more specifically, very bright) recent advances in super-bright but energy-efficient LEDs have allowed the light to be brighter, and better battery technology means that they also last much longer.

Many solar lights are designed to be pushed into the ground on stakes to light a route, but you can also buy solar security lights, lights for the shed or garage, and even pretty fairy lights that can be wound into the branches of a tree.

Shadow play

One unusual technique to consider is to make a feature of the shadows your lighting casts, rather than the objects which themselves are illuminated. This has a very sophisticated effect, but is rather easy to achieve.

It involves three elements: a light that's sufficiently bright to cast good strong shadows; a plant or object that's sufficiently interesting; and a blank canvas against which the display can be cast. The first part is straightforward, as the brightness of a light is usually fairly easy to predict from the type of bulb and its power requirements. What you choose to use as the subject matter will depend on your personal taste and the style of your garden – plants with architectural leaves, or statues with good clean lines, are both interesting options.

The third part is the only one that might be difficult to provide, as not all gardens include a blank wall, fence or similar surface. You could create one specially, though, either by clearing an existing feature or by adding a totally new one – perhaps a semi-transparent fabric screen adjacent to a seating area. A light shone past some interesting plants on to the back of such a screen would have magical effects.

Right light, right place

A common mistake when designing lighting installations is to use the wrong type of light in the wrong place. We're not just talking about making sure you use equipment that's suitable for exterior use – although that in itself is very important. On top of that you need to be sure the light fitting, and particularly the type of bulb it uses, will give a suitable effect. While bright halogen floodlights are great for illuminating an outdoor work area, or for keeping the outside of your house secure, they're far from appropriate when it comes to picking out a feature plant or softly up-lighting a statue. Ideally you should try and see what a light is like in operation before you make a purchase.

GLOSSARY, USEFUL CONTACTS, INDEX

Glossary

All-in ballast – A mix of gravel and sand used in the production of cement.

Arbour – A garden shelter most often constructed from wooden posts and beams, usually enclosing a seating area, and often used as a support for climbing plants.

Arris rail – A horizontal fencing rail with a triangular cross-section.

Balusters – The vertical elements of a balustrade.

Balustrade – A line of balusters joined together by rails at top and bottom.

Base – Term most often used to describe the sand or mortar layer on top of which paving or foundation is laid.

Basketweave – Ornamental style of bricklaying in which the bricks are laid in parallel pairs with each pair rotated 90° compared to the pair before.

Bat – A brick that's only half as long as a normal brick, and consequently often referred to as a half-brick. Used to fill the gaps at the end or corner of a wall.

Blinding – A thin layer of sharp sand raked over hardcore to fill air gaps in the surface and thereby reduce future movement and the amount of concrete required.

Bond – The pattern in which bricks are laid.

Boundary – Dividing line between properties, most often denoted by a hedge or fence.

Bull-nosed bricks – Bricks curved at one or both ends.

Butt-jointing – Method of laying stone or concrete slabs without leaving gaps between them.

Capping – A top layer of bricks, tiles or slabs that's flush with the sides of the wall.

Closeboard – Robust timber fence construction consisting of upright posts with horizontal arris rails between them, to which vertical boards are attached.

Cold frame – Small greenhouse-like structure up to about a metre tall with wooden or glass sides and an opening glass lid.

Common bricks – Cheapest variety of building brick. Generally not intended to be seen, being usually covered by render or plaster, etc.

Coping – A top layer of bricks, tiles or slabs that overhangs the wall.

Dot-and-dab – Technique of using five separate blobs of mortar (one under each corner of the slab and one in the centre) when laying tiles or slabs.

DPC – Damp-proof course, an impervious layer designed to prevent damp from the ground rising up through a wall.

Engineering bricks – Dense, very hard bricks.

English bond – Bricklaying pattern composed of alternating courses of stretchers and headers in which the latter are displaced by one half of their width, allowing them to sit centrally above the joints in the course below.

Face bricks – Better-quality bricks intended to be seen rather than covered by render or cladding.

Fall – Sloping ground surface that enables rainwater to drain away.

Family tree – Fruit tree on to which one or more branches from other types of fruit-bearing tree have been grafted.

Fedge – Term sometimes used to describe a hedge formed from fruiting plants.

Flemish bond – Bricklaying pattern made up of alternating headers and pairs of stretchers, with the courses staggered.

Flettons – Alternative name for common bricks.

Footings – Term variously used to describe holes dug in the ground to accommodate the foundations of walls, and the concrete foundations themselves.

Frog – The moulded hollow found in the surface of some bricks.

Galvanised – Protected with an outer coating of zinc.

Habit – The general shape, size and growing pattern of a plant.

Hard landscaping – An artificial area of timber or stone within a garden environment, such as a wall, fence, patio or gazebo.

Hardcore – A mixture of stones, crushed brick and concrete debris, usually recycled from a demolition site. Used in wall, path and patio foundations, etc.

Head – Height to which the water in a fountain will be lifted.

Header – The short side of a brick.

Herringbone – Bricklaying pattern in which successive courses are laid diagonally in opposite directions to create a zigzag effect.

Interwoven panel – A frame of timber used in fencing, consisting of horizontal strips of wood woven between vertical boards.

Joists – Horizontal support beams, such as those used to support decking.

Lap panel – A frame of timber used in fencing, with an infill of thin planks set so that each one overlaps the next.

Paling – A fence of irregular stakes tied to three lengths of horizontal wire and supported at intervals by strong posts.

Pergola – A covered walkway made from vertical posts supporting an open 'roof' of beams.

Picket fencing – A fence consisting of widely spaced timber nailed to two or three horizontal rails, strengthened at intervals by sturdy vertical posts.

Plate compactor – A vibrating motor attached to a large flat plate, used to compact hardcore.

Plinth bricks – Bricks with a chamfered face or edge.

Pointing – The process of neatly finishing the mortar joint between bricks in order to exclude rain.

Polytunnel – Semi-permanent polythene-covered structure used as a garden greenhouse.

Potager – A bed planted with vegetables rather than flowers.

Queen closers – Bricks cut in half along their length.

Rails – Horizontal lengths of timber such as those found in a fence or balustrade.

RCD – Residual current device, a safety device that trips a power supply if it detects a difference between negative and positive charges that is beyond acceptable safety margins.

Riser – Vertical element of a step.

Setts – Small rectangular blocks, most often granite, used in paving.

Sharp sand – A gritty sand with a low clay content, used in building (most notably for cement) and gardening. Also known as coarse sand or grit sand.

Skin – A single width of brickwork.

Soakaway – A deep hole filled with compacted gravel through which water can drain away.

Stretcher – The long side of a brick.

Stretcher bond – Pattern of laying bricks or blocks in which they're laid end to end with their long faces exposed. The courses are staggered by half a brick to avoid the joints lining up.

Sub-base – The layer of crushed, compacted material that commonly forms the lowest layer of a foundation.

Tamping down – Firmly compacting loose materials.

TPO – Tree preservation order. An order served by the local authority awarding special protection to an individual tree or a group of trees. Protected trees cannot be topped, lopped, felled, uprooted, treated or damaged without consent from the local authority.

Tread – Horizontal element of a step.

Type one (more often 'Type 1') – A specific mix of crushed brick, rock, sand and masonry dust used in the construction of foundations.

Wattle – Traditional type of fencing panel woven from strips of flexible bark and thin branches.

Useful contacts

Decking

Arbordeck
Lincoln Castle Way, New Holland,
Barrow-upon-Humber,
North Lincolnshire DN19 7RR
tel 01469 535 427
email enquiries@arbordeck.co.uk
website www.arbordeck.co.uk

Deckbuilders
The Firs, Hill, Pershore,
Worcestershire WR10 2JZ
tel 0845 370 7790
email info@deckbuildersltd.co.uk
website www.deckbuildersltd.co.uk

Garden lighting

Lighting for Gardens
7 Dunhams Court, Letchworth Garden
City, Hertfordshire SG6 1WB
tel 01462 486777
website www.lightingforgardens.com

Moonlight Design Ltd
9 Essex Road, London E4 6DG
tel 020 8925 8639
email info@moonlightdesign.co.uk
website www.moonlightdesign,co.uk

Patios

StoneFlair by Bradstone
Bardon Hall, Copt Oak Road,
Markfield, Leicestershire LE67 9PJ
tel 01335 372289
website www.aggregate.com

Plants and seeds

Marshall & Co
Alconbury Hill, Huntingdon,
Cambridgeshire PE28 4HY
tel 01480 443390
website www.marshalls-seeds.co.uk

Thompson & Morgan
Poplar Lane, Ipswich,
Suffolk IP8 3BU
tel 0844 248 5383
website www.thompson-morgan.com

Tools

Draper
Hursley Road, Chandler's Ford,
Eastleigh, Hampshire SO53 1YF
tel 023 8026 6355
website www.drapertools.com

Screwfix
Trade House, Mead Avenue,
Yeovil, Somerset BA22 8RT
tel 0500 414141
website www.screwfix.com

Water gardening

Oase Living Water
3 Telford Gate, Whittle Road,
West Portway Industrial Estate, Andover,
Hampshire SP10 3SF
tel 01264 333 225
email enquiries@oase-livingwater.com
website www.oase-livingwater.com

Tetra
PO Box 271, Southampton,
Hampshire SO18 3ZX
tel 023 8060 6070
website www.tetra-fish.co.uk

Royal Horticultural Society

80 Vincent Square, London SW1P 2PE
tel 0845 260 5000
website www.rhs.org.uk

Index

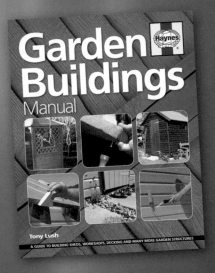

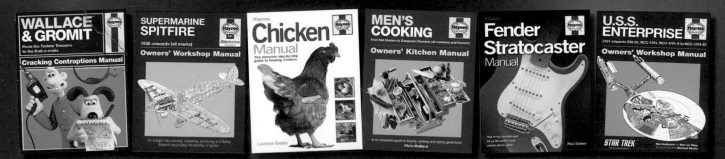